GOOGLE AND THE MYTH OF
UNIVERSAL KNOWLEDGE

[A VIEW FROM EUROPE]

GOOGLE AND THE MYTH OF UNIVERSAL KNOWLEDGE

Jean-Noël Jeanneney

TRANSLATED BY TERESA LAVENDER FAGAN

The University of Chicago Press
Chicago and London

S

303.376
JEA

The University of Chicago Press, Chicago 60637
The University of Chicago Press, Ltd., London
© 2007 by The University of Chicago
All rights reserved. Published 2007
Paperback edition 2007
Printed in the United States of America

16 15 14 13 12 11 10 09 08 07   4 5 6 7

ISBN-13: 978-0-226-39577-7 (cloth)
ISBN-13: 978-0-226-39578-4 (paper)
ISBN-10: 0-226-39577-4 (cloth)
ISBN-10: 0-226-39578-2 (paper)

Originally published as *Quand Google défie l'Europe: Plaidoyer pour un sursaut,* © Mille et une nuits, département de la Librairie Arthème Fayard, 2005.

Library of Congress Cataloging-in-Publication Data

Jeanneney, Jean Noël, 1942–
    [Quand Google défie l'Europe. English]
    Google and the myth of universal knowledge : a view from Europe / Jean–Noël Jeanneney ; translated by Teresa Lavender Fagan.
        p.   cm.
    ISBN-13: 978-0-226-39577-7 (alk. paper)
    ISBN-10: 0-226-39577-4 (alk. paper)
    1. Google. 2. Web search engines—Europe. 3. Electronic information resources—Europe. 4. Digital libraries. 5. Library materials—Digitization. 6. Libraries and the Internet. 7. Information organization. 8. Internet—Social aspects. 9. Google (Firm) 10. Internet industry—Europe. I. Title.
ZA4234.G64J4313 2007
025.04—dc22   2006019650

CONTENTS

FOREWORD

To see a World in a Grain of Sand
And a Heaven in a Wild Flower
Hold Infinity in the palm of your hand
And Eternity in an hour
:: WILLIAM BLAKE, 1803 ::

The promise of Google is as enchanting and mystical as this vision of William Blake. Everyone with access to the Internet can soon view the recorded memory of the ages in the palm of their hand and search this universe in a fraction of a second. Digitizing all the books in five major research libraries and working with other institutions to put online extensive print, cartographic, film, and other documentary materials, Google is the newest wonder of the world, a colossus spanning the continents, linking the centuries, and compressing space. And it is still in its childhood. Google, with its incredible search engine, its successful business model, and its corporate creed of "Don't be evil" is seductive to chronically underfunded libraries and archives, the custodians of our societies' cumulative documentary heritage. The potential to open the extensive, sometimes fragile holdings of these institutions for education, research, and other public uses is powerful and realizes a central goal of generations of both librarians and archivists. But is the marriage with Google worthy of their distinguished traditions and values, and is it fully in keeping with their responsibilities as stewards of one of the most significant public resources? Have they explored the implications and consequences of this approach or considered alternate paths to fulfilling their professional destiny?

Jean-Noël Jeanneney, president of the Bibliothèque nationale de France, has launched an essential international discussion. The first edition of this little volume, *Quand Google défie l'Europe: Plaidoyer pour un sursaut* (When Google challenges Europe: A wake-up call), published in France in April 2005, has substantially advanced this discussion in Europe. It has provoked serious international debate about allowing one approach to dominate in making extensive holdings of national literatures, publications, and other documents available in a global digital environment.

In challenging Google's claim that it will "organize the world's information and make it universally accessible and useful," Jeanneney, like Michael Gorman, past president of the American Library Association, notes the distinction between accessing knowledge and merely retrieving a few pages from a major book without the context of the whole. He goes even further in emphasizing context. For him the issue is not just the whole work but also the cultural context and language in which the work was conceived, written, published, read, understood, and maintained. Information has many contexts and receives its full meaning within these contexts. How a search engine selects, organizes, and presents information can destroy or invisibly distort the context. Complex cultural nuances are forced into molds and structures built by and appropriate to one dominant cultural perspective. And if that cultural perspective also determines what portion of the world's recorded knowledge is digitized and available for search on the Web, the possibilities of distortion escalate. Jeanneney has moved beyond questions of technology to identify and explore the fundamental cultural policy issues implicit in Google's massive ambition.

Jeanneney comes to this debate with the perspective of an experienced public official and historian who has been placing library issues in the context of national cultural policy for some time. His argument seems more political than professional, as librarians and archivists have traditionally approached professional discourse. It goes to the heart of the societal roles of these professions and demands that they justify themselves anew for the twenty-first century. Librarians and archivists need to shift from the usual consideration of standards and best practices to reflect on the nature of the global information infrastructure. What are the stewards of the world's documentary heritage collectively attempting to accomplish in this new environment? What is their vision for this new global information resource? This is the challenge Jeanneney has launched.

Jeanneney's initiative builds upon the "Universal Declaration on Cultural Diversity" adopted unanimously by the General Conference of UNESCO on November 2, 2001. Over the past few years, political leaders in charge of cultural policy have been developing a cultural response to the tendencies of the global economy. This debate has been largely ignored in the Anglophone world, secure in the dominance of the English language and cultural paradigm. In the United States, the issue was seen as affecting Hollywood and the entertainment industry. The UNESCO declaration, though, like Jeanneney's argument, finds deep resonance among other linguistic and cultural groups endeavoring to retain their modes of expression in this global environment. Librarians and archivists were not active in the debates leading to the declaration, but its principles and approaches have considerable relevance to their thinking on the global information infrastructure. The articles of the declaration bear directly on the values that need to be embedded in this infrastructure, as these few extracts suggest:

ARTICLE 1. As a source of exchange, innovation and creativity, cultural diversity is as necessary for humankind as biodiversity is for nature.

ARTICLE 4. The defense of cultural diversity is an ethical imperative, inseparable from respect for human dignity.

ARTICLE 6. While ensuring the free flow of ideas by word and image, care should be exercised that all cultures can express themselves and make themselves known.

ARTICLE 11. Market forces alone cannot guarantee the preservation and promotion of cultural diversity, which is the key to sustainable human development. From this perspective, the pre-eminence of public policy, in partnership with the private sector and civil society, must be reaffirmed.

Agree or disagree, the debate is central to the future of our information stewards. The capabilities of Google's search capacity and its dominant business model are challenges not only or even primarily for Europe but for librarians and archivists throughout the world. The issue is not pro- or con-Google. Google is adapting and evolving rapidly to meet some of the concerns Jeanneney raised a year ago, modifying its algorithms and expanding coverage in other languages. It will continue to develop. The fundamental issue is how best librarians and archivists can fulfill their responsibilities for the global information infrastructure.

In certain respects, Google has simply emphasized issues inherent in established methodologies for decades. Traditional library "algorithms," accessing information by author, title, and subject, have been culturally driven since Dewey, with all the biases and limitations of subject headings and ignoring the ways others, like aboriginal societies, have organized and managed traditional, often shared, knowledge systems. The archival principles of *respect des fonds* and of provenance are inherent in the nature of the record, ensuring the continuity of context and thus evidentiary value. But archival description tends to assume user knowledge of these principles, and few archives have been able to develop significant user-friendly access points. New technology and public expectation for online access, whether driven by Google, Yahoo, or the next new search engine, highlight the limitations of traditional practices. Google, forcefully representing the impatience of the marketplace, is driving the urgency of discussion and the necessity of action.

Librarians and archivists are the beneficiaries of long and distinguished professional traditions, with core values and principles honed and tested in various jurisdictions through more than a century of good and bad times. I suggest these be reexamined and their meaning understood to address the challenges of the twenty-first century. They need to be our compass as we explore the potential of the digital world. As we consider partnerships and how we make the resources entrusted to our care accessible online, I would highlight five key principles, which I believe have characterized and motivated our predecessors in building our various national and local institutions. These were discussed and adopted in principle at a meeting of several national librarians of *la francophonie* in Paris on February 28, 2006.

Librarians and archivists as stewards of significant, often unique, publicly owned information resources, should ensure that

1. public access online to such publicly owned resources will remain free; information providers may develop and charge for value-added features, but the source material should be accessible and free;
2. agreements with private-sector partners to publish or digitize significant collections will be nonexclusive in nature, in both a legal and a de facto sense;
3. the digital images will be prepared to a suitable preservation standard and maintained in the public sector with a commitment to long-term preservation and accessibility;
4. the integrity and authenticity of the original source material will be maintained and cannot be altered in the online environment;
5. as far as possible, online access will be multilingual and multicultural as appropriate for the source material.

To these one might add that librarians and archivists have a continuing professional responsibility for the selection of materials for large-scale digitization projects. Digitization strategies driven solely by the immediate marketplace or by advertisers will result in an uncoordinated patchwork of content available to the search engines. The information stewards have had and should maintain a leading role in developing worldwide collaborative initiatives for making accessible significant and relevant content sensitive to the many cultural contexts. This requires a significant professional contribution, not just unlocking the stacks to a collection originally selected for other purposes and a more limited audience.

Google, Yahoo, and search engines yet to come offer immense promise and possibilities, simplifying certain types of research, opening the contents of many libraries and archives to a broad public. Jean-Noël Jeanneney and all librarians and archivists look forward to being active partners in this international project. But it must be done with some thought not just to the immediate expectations of the market but for the future of our inherited knowledge resources. It seems a truism reiterated by countless dinner speakers that in this century, information is power. For those who would amass all the world's information, this truism needs to be tempered by Lord Acton's observation from his study of history: "Power tends to corrupt, and absolute power corrupts absolutely." In our civic affairs, democratic governments are based on the division of powers, providing suitable checks and balances for a healthy and sustainable society. In the world of the Web, should one entity dominate all aspects of content from selection to digitization, access, and preservation? And if it is sold next year, what could a new, less benign owner do with such a colossus? I would trust neither the public nor the private sector with such power. A division of powers, roles, and responsibilities, based upon tested professional principles and respecting the imperatives both of cultural diversity and of the marketplace, may be the best approach for the long term. We need balance and well-planned partnerships to achieve the real promise of the digital commons.

Jean-Noël Jeanneney has opened a debate vital to the library and archival professions and fundamental to advancing the global knowledge society.

Ian E. Wilson
LIBRARIAN AND ARCHIVIST OF CANADA
BIBLIOTHÉCAIRE ET ARCHIVISTE DU CANADA

ACKNOWLEDGMENTS

I could never have imagined writing this little book in the short period demanded by the timeliness of the subject without the support of all those—both employees of the Bibliothèque nationale de France and others—who assisted in this undertaking, provided information, and contributed their like-minded thinking. I therefore express my gratitude to Annie Lou Cot, Jean-Marie Borzeix, Denis Bruckmann, Jean-Pierre Cendron, Agnès Chauveau, Catherine Dhérent, Michel Fingerhut (whom I thank for the two quotations, one from Plato and one from Brin and Page), Renée Herbouze, Jean-Marcel Jeanneney, Hervé Le Crosnier, Catherine Lupovici, Cécile Méadel, Xavier Perrot, Agnès Saal, Jacqueline Sanson, Valérie Tesnière (who was assistant secretary-general of the French steering committee), and Caroline Wiegandt.

This book was first published in France in April 2005. The

present work, made available a little over a year later, is an updated, revised, and supplemented version intended for an English-language, specifically North American audience. I am delighted that it is being made available to those readers, and am grateful to the University of Chicago Press for publishing it. The book has been adapted to respond to specific concerns; it nevertheless remains completely faithful to the spirit of the original French publication.

Jean-Noël Jeanneney

MARCH 2, 2006

GOOGLE AND THE MYTH OF
UNIVERSAL KNOWLEDGE

INTRODUCTION

What they admired about the cedar tree was that it had been brought back in a hat. :: Gustave Flaubert, *Bouvard et Pécuchet*, chapter 1 ::

A Resounding Announcement

It all began on December 14, 2004. All of it? Not quite. Let's say that a piece of information received by the press agencies on that day convulsed our everyday lives, our activities, and our imaginations.

We learned that Google, the American company that provides the most widely used search engine for our computers, was planning over a period of six years to digitize some 15 million printed volumes, or around 4.5 billion pages.

Google's founders, Sergey Brin and Larry Page, made the announcement to great fanfare from their headquarters in

Mountain View, California. We learned that an agreement had been signed with Stanford University and the University of Michigan for their libraries to make their rich collections available to the two entrepreneurs, who were eager to reproduce them by scanning the books (by OCR, optical character recognition) and then distributing them over the Internet. We knew no details of those contracts, which had been negotiated in great secret, but their spirit was clear. The idea was to offer, gratis, online, all works no longer in copyright and to give limited access to all others published since 1923.

Three other prestigious institutions were involved to a lesser extent. The Widener Library at Harvard and the New York Public Library had pledged to provide some tens of thousands of works on behalf of this vast undertaking. It was clear from their modest offers that they were being cautious, but equally clear that they approved, since they had committed themselves.

This was obviously an American project, but one that reached out to the British. The Bodleian Library at Oxford, we were told, would also contribute, with works published before 1900. So the proposal was taking a symbolic slant. We saw the familiar Anglo-Saxon solidarity: to borrow Churchill's comment to de Gaulle, one of the leading universities in Great Britain was ready, without consulting anyone on the other side of the English Channel, to look out over the "open main" rather than turn toward the Continent in search of European patriotism for the adventure under way.

Of course, the announcement to the world at large of this Pharaonic project—then known as Google Print for Libraries or, less formally, Google Library—still left many unanswered questions, notably regarding the technical procedures envisioned, the ponderous logistics to be put into place, the durability of the products of digitization, the system of financing, respect for the rights of authors and publishers. But despite all the glossing and even bragging, for those paying close attention the announcement appeared monumental.

A Healthy Jolt

As I've often said, responding to questions from various media about my reaction as head of the Bibliothèque nationale de France, as a historian, as a citizen, as a European, I experienced neither distress nor irritation at the project. Just a healthy jolt. Out of which two simple convictions were immediately born.

First, there was satisfaction at what appeared to be the realization of an old dream that had been developing gradually with advancing technologies, the dream that a treasure trove of knowledge, accumulated for centuries, would be opened up to the benefit of all, and primarily to those whose family, sociological, or geographical situation deprived them of easy access to the cultural and intellectual legacy of humanity.

Yet at the same time I was seized by anxiety. It seemed necessary at all costs to understand how this daunting undertaking, now whetting our appetite, would be structured. I was reminded of Cyrano, Edmond Rostand's hero, standing under Roxane's balcony and feverishly calling out his love for her: "I will throw them to you in clumps without making a bouquet." Cyrano, who was distraught, played with such disorder in order to seduce. But in the case we are dealing with here, the clumps have no sense, and only bouquets have value. An indeterminate, disorganized, unclassified, uninventoried profusion is of little interest.

In spite of what nineteenth-century publishers sometimes imagined, there can be no universal library, only specific ways of looking at what is universal. Choices are always made, and must be made. Since the time of Gutenberg, the books produced by the human race (and I am speaking only of those printed in the West) amount to more than one hundred million.

The quantity promised by Google, so impressive in absolute terms, corresponds to only a small percentage of this huge total. So we must wonder what books will be chosen, what criteria will determine the list. And if Google, aware of these questions, announces an (uncertain) plan of classification, the debate on its validity and its potential imperialism is not only legitimate but essential, since such a plan risks being imposed at the expense of centuries of intellectual wisdom.

Let's go even further. As anyone who uses Google knows, what is intrinsic to all the information it provides is hierarchization. Even if there are many pages of results, the searcher rarely goes beyond the first few. This is the marketing principle of what large commercial enterprises call the "gondola end." The goods that are offered are not placed haphazardly. The thinking behind their selection is essential, for it amounts to a sanctioning of their relative importance.

Two impulses are at work here at the same time: the cultural impulse and the commercial impulse. On the one hand, the pervading intellectual climate will help determine the principles of selection and, to an even greater extent, the principles by which those choices are classified and indexed. On the other, the profit motive will necessarily promote one product over another. Many Europeans, however, refuse to accept that a cultural work might be considered and treated as just another piece of merchandise.

We are faced with several possible dangers: with respect to works of various cultural heritages that have fallen into the public domain, the list of priorities will likely weigh in favor of Anglo-Saxon culture. With respect to works still under copyright, of which only excerpts, or "snippets," will be offered for the time being, the weight of American publishers may be overwhelming. As for journals and books disseminating ongoing research, the dominance of work from the United States may become even greater than it is today.

What is at stake is language, of course, and we can see how the use of English (in its American form) threatens to become ever more prevalent at the expense of other European languages—all of them. Radio is protected by language, as, in part, is television (especially the news). For the Web the risk is even greater, for although users tend to prefer messages in their own language, by consulting a written text on the screen they are encouraging concession to the current lingua franca, that more or less simplified English which, if not contained, will become ever more dominant.

I am thinking of all European languages here, while not minimizing the importance of this quarrel for the French language and Francophone countries; the support of the nations who ally themselves to us, especially our cousins in Canada, will be essential. But the Francophone issue is not the only one on the front lines of this indispensable effort. We must at all costs, with the same thrust and equal ardor, defend the other European languages bearing diverse and complementary cultures.

Likewise, we must attach particular importance to the digitization of the numerous translations that have long been published within our continent and that continue to be produced in spite of rising costs. Every work written in a language of our twenty-five countries and translated into another should automatically find a place on our lists of selections, once we've created the means to establish such lists—being chosen for translation is in itself a mark of a work's significance.

One question has been raised that the top executives of Google have themselves commented on (especially since our initial reactions): Why do we assume that the works of our civilizations, which have fed that of the United States, will not be taken into consideration in their appropriate places on the lists of selected titles? I don't, in fact, believe there will be any deliberate ostracism or censure, but I do believe there is an overall inclination, a leaning, a spontaneous tendency that necessarily leads to an imbalance.

It's worth noting that although works originally written in English are widely offered in European languages, translations undertaken across the Atlantic are extremely rare: translations account for less than 3 percent of everything published in the United States. This, too, is an effect of dominance, with that conscious or unconscious arrogance that results from it and a spontaneous prioritizing of things that fit into the American vision of the world.

This will assuredly remain the case, whatever the future holds, so long as we ourselves, on the eastern side of the Atlantic, have not made the effort to digitize our intellectual and cultural treasures, using budgets geared less toward consumers and the market (whose strength is irresistible only if we allow it to be) than toward the interests of our citizens.

Brush Fire

I might have hesitated to brandish this European banner had I not realized very quickly how Google's project, once its ramifications had been clarified, concerned both the sensibilities and the civic-mindedness of European citizens. Breaking a rather lengthy silence, on Saturday, January 22, 2005, I contributed an article to the editorial pages of *Le Monde* entitled "Quand Google défie l'Europe" (the title of the original French edition of the present work), which outlined the motives and what was at stake in this call to action. In the days that followed, there were very few reactions, but when I had the opportunity to speak of the affair again in front of reporters—at a gathering held to announce the ambitious plan by the Bibliothèque nationale to digitize French daily newspapers since the nineteenth century—and then to return to the subject the following morning in an interview on the radio station France

Inter with Stéphane Paoli, it seemed I'd ignited a brush fire.

I was solicited by reporters day after day, week after week, while the issue was heating up in all our neighboring countries—Germany, Italy, Spain, Ireland, and Great Britain—where the press and Web sites were publishing numerous articles, but also in Japan, Canada, and even the United States. Interest was being shown in Brussels, at the European Commission and the European Parliament, prompted in particular by the charismatic Olivier Duhamel, who until quite recently was still a deputy in the Parliament and was among the very first to get behind this cause. During the same period I received many encouraging e-mail messages, offers of help, and constructive criticism.

I was beginning to be surprised at the silence of politicians in France, when Jacques Chirac, president of the Republic, first approached me through his advisers, then asked me to meet with him and the minister of culture and communication on March 16 at the Elysée Palace. Informing the press of this meeting, President Chirac announced that he would sponsor an initiative, requesting the support of several European partner countries. And he asked me to actively pursue the undertaking and to come up with a possible strategy.

With that word coming from the top, the affair leapt to the front pages of the newspapers. A public debate began in Europe, and, as we could tell from activity on the Web, it was a debate in which many people in the United States were interested as well. The first edition of this little book, written in three weeks in March 2005 and published in April, was meant to fuel the debate, sound the alarm, and get people moving.

Europe on the March

Since that time, I believe, the conviction that fired me and the appeal that I launched have lost nothing of their legitimacy, necessity, or urgency.

Evidence of what is at stake, which had struck me so strongly during the first months of the controversy, and the certainty that the issue was something that would affect minds and hearts, have persistently been reinforced. I have continued to receive dozens of requests for interviews from newspapers and from radio and television stations worldwide, not only in France or Europe, but from every continent. The analyses and commentaries that have appeared in the traditional media as well as on the Web constitute an impressive mass of documents. A translation of the present book is already available in German; another has appeared in Arabic thanks to the director of the Library of Alexandria, whose essential role in the service of the values we share I discuss later in these pages; and others have been published in Chinese and Portuguese (Brazil). Translations will soon be available in Italy and in several Spanish-speaking countries in Latin America.

The leaders of the five nations solicited by Jacques Chirac — Germany, Spain, Italy, Poland, and Hungary (at that time Gerhard Schroeder, Jose Luis Rodriguez Zapatero, Silvio Berlusconi, Aleksander Kwasniewski, and Ferenc Gyurcsany) — immediately agreed to sign a letter with him dated April 28, 2005, which called upon the authorities in Brussels to join our initiative. As of May 2, 2005, during the European meetings on culture held in Paris, both the president of the European Council, Jean-Claude Juncker, and the president of the Commission, José Manuel Barroso, lent solid support to this project by delivering their prepared speeches with an unmistakable tone of personal enthusiasm. At the same time, twenty-two out of the twenty-four national libraries in the European Union signed the motion I had proposed, which asserted a commonality of conviction and determination. Later, speaking to my counterparts from all over the world in Oslo on August 17, and then to those in Europe in Luxembourg on September 27, I found attentive audiences. Their invaluable observations and suggestions refined and deepened my thinking. I could then see that the rejection of the European Constitution by France and the Netherlands during the referenda of May and June, harmful as it might be for the Union, was not as detrimental to our present concern as might have been feared. On the contrary, some members seemed to harbor the idea that a great shared cultural project—though not repairing the damage done by the "No"—would mean that there was still hope for progress, particularly in the realm of culture, where cooperation has historically been difficult.

Nothing could have given us greater encouragement. I seized any opportunity offered me to spread the good word to the most diverse audiences in France, Belgium, Germany, Italy, and wherever possible.

Meanwhile, in the United States . . .

Meanwhile, as may well be imagined, we were very attentive to developments in the United States.

In May 2005, Google placed on the Web the first works offered within the framework of its program. Their quality was often mediocre, no doubt because the job had been done too quickly. The inevitable American self-centering of the selections was immediately apparent.

At the Bibliothèque nationale we had fun seeing what could be found by typing in the names of Victor Hugo, Dante, Cervantes, and Goethe. We found that only English-language publications were offered. (To be fair, for Hugo—oddly—a publication in German was listed). Granted, in the French version of the pilot site, things have somewhat improved, our escapades having perhaps triggered an effort to digitize a number of well-known Francophone works. But the problem was shunted elsewhere, and Internet users were not given the means to understand the general workings of the system. In February

2006, for example, a search for Cervantes on the Spanish site of Google Book Search (book.google.es) curiously first brought up five works in French, followed by three books in English, before, in the ninth and final position, there appeared a collection of excerpts from *Don Quixote* in the author's own language.

The concern about Google's initiative expressed very early by the American Library Association (which I shall mention later) was soon joined by complaints from publishers (university presses at first, then others). These publishers noted that Google was about to put their books online without having sought permission, merely announcing that works under copyright would not be used. I heard the same sentiments at the Frankfurt Book Fair when I was asked, on October 21, 2005, to present our ideas before an audience of attentive professionals of all nationalities, notably Americans (who were particularly virulent). They were hardly civil to the representative from Google, who once again came to explain, with that familiar naïveté, his satisfaction at being able to benefit humanity while making a lot of money.

So the protests voiced in the United States joined up with those from France and elsewhere in Europe. During the same period, several powerful companies expressed their intent to enter the fray, including Yahoo, in association with a project called Open Content Alliance, ostensibly respectful of the experience of libraries; and Microsoft, which in November signed an agreement with the British Library for the promised upcoming digitization of some hundred thousand works.

Under these conditions, Google announced, on August 11, 2005, a unilateral and ambiguous moratorium on its digitization plans. Curiously, it invited publishers—in a sort of reverse reading of the law—to let it know, before November, which works should not be digitized. Google's decision to temporarily halt its plans was limited in practical terms, but it appeared important in symbolic terms, which of course I emphasized in the press. Soon afterwards, Google Library was renamed Google Book Search—as if it were necessary to signal a new departure following the initial missteps.

The Lines Are Drawn

As autumn progressed, it became imperative, once the major principles had been presented, to define the concrete components of our undertaking. In Paris, a steering committee was established under the direction of the minister of culture, Renaud Donnedieu de Vabres (with myself as vice-president), charged with reviewing and distilling, as quickly as possible, any suggestions the French contingent might offer to our partners. Representatives from the various professional areas concerned worked with us, and we obtained good results. But we were careful to maintain close contact with other large libraries, for although we hoped to feed the debate, we never conceived of proceeding exclusively on our own.

This initial work has been completed, sanctioned by a report by the minister of culture to a council of ministers on February 8. It was first necessary for the French case (and we hope others will do the same) to give an overview of the situation and to inventory all the digitization that has been accomplished to date at the initiative of all sorts of associations—universities, museums, and so forth—while pointing out that although we aren't starting from scratch, we have to avoid the temptation of bestowing such an elegant name as European Digital Library upon the disparate collection of existing digital projects. We are dealing, of course, with an entirely different dimension.

It was then essential to specify the potential cost of the hitherto unknown digitization of books carried out on such a large scale. Since December 14, 2004, fanciful and contradictory figures have been quoted from a vast range of sources. So at the end of 2005 we launched an investigation. With the help of IBM, a consultant chosen for the quality of its proposal, we asked for competitive bids from those companies that might hope to obtain all or part of the European market (a good number of them had been talking to us since the summer): the results will soon be available.

While this was going on, the Bibliothèque nationale started working up a financing plan—both the necessary budget and the way in which its weight might be distributed. The European Commission—which has issued a helpful appeal for ideas on this subject within the framework of a plan for 2010—has refused for the time being, as was stressed by Viviane Reding, European commissioner for Information Society and Media, to contribute directly to digitization. It is a refusal that I believe should be reconsidered, not only for practical but also for symbolic reasons. By spreading the financial burden among the European Union and its member states we would better show that this truly is a common endeavor: not only to finance the digitization of collections belonging to the various EU states, but also to consolidate a common European cultural heritage. A gathering of the EU ministers of culture, in Brussels on November 14, revealed that in this respect the various countries were still divided in their points of view. The reticent ones will have to be rallied.

The principle of "reinforced cooperation" now in effect in Europe might very well apply here: we could begin with the first countries ready to go forward in concert and at the same pace, while extending a welcome to all those who might like to join us.

A good way to convince them, of course, is to proceed with collective thinking about the criteria for choosing and organizing the works to be digitized. This is more important than ever. It is imperative that Europeans work together to construct the entirety of their offering on the basis of well thought-out and explicit principles, thus showing the way, like Ariadne's thread, through our vast literary heritage. As for the second part of the equation, the books and journals still under copyright, cooperation with publishers responsible both to their own interests and to those of their authors must be at the heart of any undertaking. We will work closely with them.

We have also been in contact with high-tech organizations in the realms of metadata, the circulation of information, and the durability of data supports. Through joint efforts, France and Germany have just launched the Quaero project (*quaero* is Latin for "I seek"), introduced in April 2005 by Gerhard Schroeder and Jacques Chirac and designed to support technological innovation in matters concerning indexing and search engines for multimedia. We are working profitably with its developers in connection with our own projects.

Realism and Promptness

As the public debate continues, we must clearly distinguish the issue of digitization from that of access to the wealth of offerings proposed.

The former calls for a budgetary plan for the coming years. The exact sums cannot be determined until we have the results of the bids (mentioned above) and know the budgets that might be contributed by state governments and by the EU, reinforced, I hope, by generous private contributions. The goal is not to increase quantities, not to provide bulk information, but to propose, as will be seen, a collection assembled according to well-considered and productive guidelines. A collection whose permanence will be guaranteed over the long term, as only public institutions can promise and ensure.

As for access, it must be widely available to all engines, according to modalities yet to be defined—unlike Google, which unabashedly reserves for itself the exclusivity of its offer. A specific European search engine dedicated to the BNE (Bibliothèque numérique européenne—European Digital Library) would offer service of a quality that a general-interest engine could not provide—for example, multilingual searches in a single request. But it will discover its full potential only if, while organizing the indexing of our cultural wealth in a truly useful, rigorously reasoned way, it authorizes all possible connections with any site that wishes free access to it.

We must now build a structure that will be both the agent for and the guarantor of this splendid ambition. May we be protected against potential administrative weights that might slow us down and hinder us. The recent months—unsurprisingly—have revealed or highlighted perils and obstacles, but this has only helped to illuminate the dimensions of the challenge. If you believe in Europe's enduring influence, indispensable for our collective pride and the balance of the planet, if you (and there are many of you in America, as well!) fervently wish for a multipolarity of cultural heritages, then you are summoned, in response to this call, to expend your energy and to manifest your commitment without delay. For although there is still time, it will soon be too late.

1

REMARKABLE PROGRESS

"We hear the breathing of the horses of space,
Pulling the wagon that we cannot see"
:: VICTOR HUGO, *Les Contemplations*, VI, 16 ::

A Positive Outlook

What we should *not* be feeling at this point is gloom. Optimism is much more appropriate. There is nothing more foolish than to deplore the progress offered by the Internet. Let's leave that to malcontents and people living in the past.

Numerous sociological studies have been published dealing with the way the Internet affects the behavior of its users. Some studies point to the risk of isolation, of discouraging the sociability inherent in research. But reflection and writing are always at some point solitary activities. I'm particularly aware of what the Internet offers many researchers and citizens, enabling them to escape an enforced isolation—those whose place in society, in the world, in the economic hierarchy of nations keeps them at a distance from the mainstream.

Like everyone else, I am aware of the profusion of information, the treasures of every kind that, thanks to the Internet, are already offered up to our appetites on our computer screens. (I am not speaking here of the more private use of the Internet, of e-mail and instant messaging, important as they are, but only of the Web in the strict sense of the term.)

France is practically the only European country—for the moment—to have decided to digitize a large number of complete works. We have lowered our sights from the unrealistic goals expressed by some when François Mitterrand, then president of the Republic, announced on July 14, 1988, the plan for a "Very Great Library . . . of an entirely new kind." The majestic building on the Seine upstream from Notre-Dame offers its thirteen million volumes to readers who prefer works produced on paper. But at the time I am writing, there are also eighty thousand books from the Banff collections (in addition to seventy thousand images and several dozen hours of sound recordings), which anyone, anywhere on the planet, can read on his or her monitor and print out, thanks to Gallica (http://gallica.bnf.fr), our virtual library, which is constantly being expanded and offers a vast range of interesting and unusual materials.

Conceived as a national and encyclopedic collection, Gallica includes monographs and periodicals; texts by classical or lesser-known authors from antiquity to the twentieth century; dictionaries; bibliographical and critical resources; publications of scholarly societies; and multimedia thematic collections concerning, for example, travels in France, Italy, and Africa—as well as a collection of documents (established with the cooperation of the Library of Congress) showcasing the French presence in North America from the time of Christopher Columbus to the nineteenth century.

Other countries have preferred, so far, to concentrate their efforts on documents of a different kind. Do you want to read Shakespeare's *Hamlet* in the first quarto edition of 1603? You have only to go to the British Library site and click on the heading "Treasures in Full." Do you need to consult a Finnish journal for a certain date in 1805? Go to the University of Helsinki Library site and the appropriate issue will appear on your screen. To consult descriptions of monuments in Egypt and Nubia, click on the site of the Maison de l'Orient et de la Méditerranée. And so forth.

Such initiatives are increasing. The Ministry of Culture has registered nearly thirty French libraries that are embarking on the digital adventure. The site of the European national libraries, TEL (The European Library), which has eighteen full members, has just opened; its purpose is to keep an up-dated list of digitized materials, to provide catalogs, and to maintain links with these. Museums, archives (the Archives of France and the Archives of Canada have just opened a common site), and the most dynamic national and university libraries around the world have developed programs of this type and are continually expanding them. The Joconde database lists eighteen thousand works from the national collections; the Enluminures database includes eighty thousand images drawn from medieval manuscripts, all of which are accessible over the Internet. There is also the "Cultural Material Alliance" program headed by the Research Library Group, and the recently opened European platform MICHAEL, piloted in France by the Ministry of Culture, which brings together the public and the private sectors.

Another program in the development stage is Cairn, both a portal of access to printed journals in the social sciences and a structure for managing journals in digital form; it will be able to handle at least twelve hundred titles (www.Cairn. info). I decided to have journals in the Bibliothèque nationale added to Cairn's collections; thus Francophones now have a counterpart to such services as the JSTOR database, which for a fee provides access to back issues of more than six hundred exclusively Anglophone journals. MathDoc, located in Grenoble, has become a valuable tool for mathematicians.

Similarly flourishing is the digitization of leaflets, "underground literature," which escape the channels of commercial publishing, and of other unique forms of testimony to our historical past and cultural vitality: engravings, ancient maps, charters or treaties, coins and medals, musical scores, photographs, oral archives, sound recordings, and so on.

The Library of Congress is playing a significant role in this respect: it has concentrated its efforts (not without narcissism, but who is entirely free of that?) on a collection entitled "American Memory," which claims to be a documentary reflection of "historical events, people, places and ideas that continue to shape America." Closely connected with that program, "Global Gateway" (part of which is being developed in cooperation with several countries) is concerned with influences from abroad. As mentioned above, I took the initiative to ensure France's involvement by signing an agreement in Paris with the Librarian of Congress, James H. Billington. We were in the midst of the Iraq controversy, and I had no regrets about demonstrating that long-term cooperation, resisting the vagaries of politics, could still be established between our two countries, which have been friends for so long.

The Book Will Survive

Optimism in the face of so many positive undertakings that were unthinkable for earlier generations need not go into mourning for the demise of books in the traditional form they have maintained since the birth of the printing press. Each time a new medium has appeared, we have seen prophets of doom announce the inevitable disappearance of what came before. At the time of the July Monarchy, proponents of elitist publications were filled with distaste and concern as they witnessed the growth of widely circulated popular dailies. In the period between the two World Wars, newspapers were scared to death by the rise of radio, to the point of refusing to be quoted in press reviews read over the airwaves. In the 1950s the development of television caused many people to predict the collapse of radio—which was saved almost immediately by the invention of the portable transistor radio. And I can still hear the fear of those who predicted, around 1984 or 1985 when I was director of Radio France, the French public radio station, that the new morning television shows were going to destroy our programming at the very time when most of our listeners tuned in; we now know that nothing of the kind happened. There are many other similar examples.

On each of these occasions, the harbingers of doom were blind to the diversity of social practices and cultural behaviors, to the complex interweaving of attitudes, to the predictable reaction of an audience that is inclined, after a detour through new channels of information, to return to a more classic medium, which it might even have ignored without that unexpected inducement. I'll wager that many Internet users will likewise be led back to classic book culture.

The Web can certainly bring back to light, even to wide circulation, works that have been lost in the recesses of bookstacks, perhaps because they are rare, difficult, or simply forgotten. Without doubt, "on demand" printing—the manufacture of single copies of published works, bound in their original format (the Bibliothèque nationale plans a similar process for sound recordings in the public domain)—will increase. We may see more reprints of obscure works in small quantities, made

21

available by current printing technology. Thanks to the Web, with the splendid diversity of its offerings, such works will gain notoriety, prompting readers to ask for them in printed form. Surveys of Gallica users have shown that many searches lead to the purchase of the work in question, either new or used, in online or traditional bookstores.

After all, the many images now reproduced—whether paintings, photographs, drawings, maps, or engravings—far from diminishing the impact of the originals, encourage people to go see them in museums; their affective power can only be enhanced by their having been previously studied. As far as I know, the imaginary museum so dear to André Malraux not only failed to alienate people who enjoyed going to exhibitions but increased their numbers throughout Europe, especially in France.

People won't forgo the convenience of having a volume within easy reach; nor will the emotion of touching books, having direct contact with the originals, their appearance, their smell, be diminished. This is something that the people who four or five years ago lost a lot of money on "e-books"—electronic books that could be downloaded for a fee and read on portable computer screens adapted for the purpose, and which suffered a resounding (if temporary) failure—just didn't understand. No doubt the idea will be reborn in another form (our Gallica library is already often used in this way and downloaded) as soon as a special tool is no longer required, but I can't believe it will ever replace the books on our shelves or on those of our children.

So I remain unperturbed by the reproaches or regrets that are sometimes voiced: "Why didn't we devote the billions of francs spent to build the Very Great Library on a major effort to digitize all that we are uselessly saving on paper!" I could point out that when the library was conceived, neither technology nor public opinion were ready for mass digitization. But there is really no dilemma here. A civilization must be able to move forward on both paths. François Mitterrand, who launched the effort, and who for a time promoted and embodied the idea of the modernity of the virtual, was also a passionate lover of books, which he enjoyed, if I may say so, with almost visceral pleasure.

The Need for Librarians and Booksellers

We may conclude, then, that neither librarians nor booksellers need worry about their possible disappearance.

The social and cultural function of librarians will be increasingly important and prestigious in the future; they will be even more useful to the public, and their profession will become more satisfying. For years, a common perception, maintained by various stereotypes, has tended to reduce the role of librarians to that of providing books, images, recordings, and other documents. In reality, librarians have always helped to organize chaos, to guide readers to the information they are seeking among the vast quantity of sources and media that contain it. And now, with the irruption of digitization, this essential function will be enhanced, and librarians should benefit from renewed recognition. More than ever before, they will stand beside professors and schoolteachers as essential intermediaries of knowledge.

As for traditional booksellers, they, too, should be confident in their future. They must of course learn to adapt, to become even better guides and intercessors. But we will discover an ever-increasing need for their contribution. On condition, of course, that the government protect them from the effects of "remaindering," which might, as happened for records, be practiced to their detriment by large anonymous chains or on-line bookstores.

In short, while a little digitization distances us from the

intermediaries of knowledge, a lot of digitization will bring us closer to them. The profusion of questionable, partisan, bizarre assertions spreading over the Web will demand sources for validation that librarians and booksellers are especially qualified to provide. The new technology can promote all sorts of newly discovered connections, productive analogies, unexpected encounters, unusual speed in the circulation of ideas and the development of inspiration. Uncontrolled, however, it can lead us astray and ultimately render us impotent.

These are intellectual concerns, but they impinge on our moral and civic life as well. Librarians will be at the forefront of those who serve this virtual impulse by constantly reminding us that knowledge must be arranged on the basis of global considerations, collective reasoning, and blended perspectives, rather than by encyclopedic listings. Not only is an understanding of the history of our cultures at stake, but also their vitality in the here and now.

I hope it's now clear why I quickly took issue with those who interpreted my position as being hostile to Google. I'm not criticizing Google's search engine, for it functions according to its own logic and owes its success to the remarkable talent of its founders. My intent has always been to prod European inertia in the face of a challenge of such dimensions—the formidable ambivalence of a marvelous invention, the World Wide Web.

2

AT THE MERCY OF THE MARKET

Virtues are lost in personal interest, as rivers are lost in the sea.
:: La Rochefoucauld, *Maximes*, 171 ::

On Google's Corporate Information page we find this boast: "Google's mission is to organize the world's information." While certainly not insincere, these words prompt us to take a closer look.

In France, no one has forgotten a recent statement by Patrick Le Lay, the CEO of TF1, the first commercial television station in the country, and the astonishment aroused, not so much by its truth as by its frankness: "TF1's mission is to help Coca-Cola, for example, sell its product. Now, for a commercial message to be received, the viewer's brain must be available to it. The mission of our programs is to make those brains available, to amuse them, to relax them between two commercials so as to make them receptive. What we are selling to Coca-Cola is available human brain time."

I am recalling Le Lay's words not to re-ignite civic indignation, which was certainly justified, but because it provides an enlightening comparison to the Web.

The "Invisible Hand"

It's instructive to look at the effects, in the world of culture, of putting one's faith in market forces alone.

I was amused to hear that one of the executives at Google bore the name of Adam Smith, the famous eighteenth-century British economist, author of *The Wealth of Nations* and inventor of the theory of the "invisible hand." According to Smith, as we know, the sum total of self-interested actions of individuals and businesses is destined, according to a strange and improbable alchemy, to spontaneously create the best of all possible worlds.

On the whole, Europe does not subscribe to that article of faith. Europeans remember what Charles de Gaulle told his minister and confidant Alain Peyrefitte on December 12, 1962: "The market has some good points. It keeps people on their toes, it rewards the best. But at the same time it creates injustices, establishes monopolies, favors cheaters. So don't be blind to the market. You mustn't imagine that it alone will solve all problems. The market isn't above the nation and the state. It's up to the state, the nation, to *keep an eye* on the market."

Europe is in a good position (as are poor countries) to know that the United States doesn't hesitate, when it suits it, to bend important rules for the sake of the market. So the government protects American farmers. It defends and promotes American airplanes when they are for sale. The Internet was not born of an ever-fecund capitalism but from the combination of military interests and "academic" imaginations. Then, in the early 1990s on our own continent, the work of CERN (Conseil/ Organisation européenne de recherche nucléaire), under the impetus of a Briton, Tim Berners-Lee, and without a commercial objective in immediate view, succeeded in establishing the World Wide Web.

Even Google, which nevertheless seems to embody the energy of the market alone, was born in 1998 at Stanford University in California, where Brin and Page were students in computer science. Initially it received federal funding, notably from the National Science Foundation and the Digital Library Initiative. This is too often forgotten; it was only later, when the business became profitable, that it centered its development on profits, with the support of venture capital.

Google's dominant philosophy is still that of short-term profit, intended to ensure revenue for shareholders. This philosophy, fortunately, is not ours—not, at least, the one that the French Left would ratify, nor those on the Right who, attentive to de Gaulle's legacy, reject American liberalism of the Chicago-school type. Some subscribe to it, of course, but in France and probably in the rest of Europe they are clearly in the minority.

Film and Audiovisuals

Two precedents are highly informative.

Let's look first at the history of radio between the two World Wars. There are two contrasting models from that time. In the United States, very early on, it was determined that the entire broadcasting industry should be developed through private investment alone, with public authority limited to dividing up frequencies. In Great Britain, by contrast, it was determined that the BBC, the voice of the nation (if not of the government), should be responsible for all programing. On the one side, after World War II, slavish attention was paid to the polls that had just appeared and were enjoying increasing use, thanks to the talent of George Gallup; on the other, polls were treated with supreme contempt. On the one side was certainty that democracy requires satisfying the immediate, currently fashionable tastes of the public; on the other, willingness to gamble with the long term by offering programs that the public can't know it will like since it doesn't yet know they exist. On the one side, financing through advertising income; on the other, through public subventions. On the one side, funding at the expense of consumers; on the other, at that of taxpayers.

During the same period, and without taking a doctrinaire approach, France established a tentative system in which the public and private sectors were combined, the state setting the bar high, the private sector demonstrating an energy fueled by competition that discouraged bureaucratic lethargy. After 1986, when television came to shake up the audiovisual world, this principle was again in force and has remained so, with a struggle, ever since.

In the case of the Web in the United States, as we know, the state seems to play an even lesser role than it has done for audiovisuals; broadcast frequencies are a moot point—on the Web there's no danger of running out of frequencies, for there's an almost infinite capacity for expansion. So public oversight is limited to the rarely exercised right to prohibit a site that violates the rules of intellectual property or that gives information useful to terrorists. (I should point out, for the record, that Washington can be very aggressive when it comes to maintaining its exclusive if quite unjustifiable control over the distribution, management, and administration of the names of domains and sites; this was evident during the Tunis summit in November 2005.)

The history of the cinema after the war is also enlightening. In 1946 the socialist leader Léon Blum went to Washington on behalf of the French government to negotiate agreements with Secretary of State James F. Byrnes in preparing for the Marshall Plan. "I'm a man who was raised with more of a taste for the theater than for the cinema," Blum later explained. He opened French screens widely to American films, which French audiences welcomed at first since they had been deprived of entertainment during the four years of the Occupation. Only after violent reaction from those involved in French cinema — Jean Marais and Madeleine Sologne, the famous couple from *L'Éternel retour* marching in the streets at the head of an impressive demonstration—was a restriction imposed, then strengthened: beginning in 1948, a quota of 121 American films per year was fixed, along with the obligation for movie theaters to show French films for at least five weeks in every three-month period. These rigorous measures saved an inventive and strong French cinema.

Now this is where a major difference with the Web arises: a system of quotas is, by nature, impossible on the Web. An Israeli recently quoted for me this passage from the Talmud: "Even if a library is filled to the point of bursting, books will always make room and will always find a place for a new arrival; this unto eternity." While often not the case with our own bookshelves, it's certainly true of the Web. Any defensive strategy is out of the question. And that's fine. For rather than building walls of protection around ourselves (however legitimate they may be for a time), being on the offensive always brings out the best in us.

The protectionist measures in themselves would have been insufficient in the case of French cinema if the state had not taken a more positive step: it established an innovative system of financial aid that allowed money and special taxes to support the industry without constricting it. Without that system, the cinema in France would be dead, or moribund, just as it has died out (temporarily, one hopes) among many of our European neighbors.

Overwhelming Advertising

Let's turn to an extremely important issue: the weight of advertising on Google's search engine. In the case of an engine driven only by the profit motive, hence by the attraction of what is statistically most profitable, the effect of advertising on the content must be examined. Recall that until now—and this is not irrelevant—books have been the only medium that has never included advertising (except that of the publisher for itself).

Google's modus operandi does not involve the insertion of advertising space similar to that found in newspapers and magazines. Internet users would pay little attention to such ads. An original and very clever—I'm tempted to say cunning—procedure has been adopted, something like the spots on commercial TV that are adapted to certain popular programs, notably sports coverage. Google sells an advertising link to interested companies, which appears on the right (or at the top) of the screen, based on the response to user queries provided on the left. These notices are especially likely to catch the attention of Internet users, since by definition they are targeted to their specific interests.

The advertising spots are sold by auction, so the richest companies have the best chance of getting even richer. A clear explanation of this commercial practice can be found on the page http://www.google.com/ads/ under the heading "Google AdWords."

The risk is threefold. First, an increasing industrial concentration could benefit the largest corporations at the expense of those that are currently more modest but are innovative and may well influence the future. Giving priority to large, established corporations is contrary to the spirit that initially created the effectiveness of the Web; it is a conservative, backward-looking system in a universe that could claim to be at the forefront of the virtual movement. Second, with respect to the international market, there is a risk that American companies, which sell at long distances, will win out at the expense of European companies, which are slower to pay their share. Finally, specifically concerning books and images, there is the danger that cultural populism will organize channels of access in favor of the most elementary, the least disturbing, and most commonplace products.

If we apply this same system to the digitization of books, we might expect there to be much less commercial pressure. The current information we are receiving on Google Book Search leaves many unanswered questions. The visit I received from several Google executives after the beginning of my campaign didn't do much to reassure me.

The company indicates that it won't—for the time being—charge for links with online bookstore sites (even with their rival, Amazon), with nearby stores, or with libraries. But it doesn't hide the fact that the profit motive will continue to dominate, following the same principle as for the rest of its activities. What pays for the digitization of materials are linked advertisements from companies that have an interest in associating their image with old or recent works likely to promote that image. As a result, books will necessarily be hierarchized in favor of those best suited to satisfy the demands of advertisers—again, chosen according to the principle of the highest bidder.

I wouldn't want to see—though I'm amused by the thought—the text of Saint-Exupéry's *Le Petit prince* accompanied by an ad for a sheep merchant, Proust's *À la Recherche du temps perdu* by an ad for a manufacturer of madeleines, *Don Quixote* by an ad for a windmill manufacturer, or Andersen by an ad for a company that sells matches. Am I exaggerating? Can we be sure this won't occur?

In France it's long been considered risky to introduce advertising for books on TV (at least, on the general-interest channels). So far, we have been lucky enough to protect ourselves against this practice, precisely to prevent best-sellers from crushing innovative, scholarly-oriented literature, the kind that temporarily reaches a restricted audience but will nourish future cultural holdings. (In the same spirit, a law sponsored by the French minister of culture, Jack Lang, and passed on 31 July 1982, set a fixed price for books, and limited discounts to 5 percent, to protect high-quality bookstores from the assault of large chains, which were planning to engage in remainder sales and thus discount everything. These measures have been largely successful.)

Let us not succumb to the illusion that those who use Google can easily distinguish between "objective" information and advertising. A survey of twenty-two thousand adults, conducted in the United States by Pew Internet and American Life Project and published in January 2005, found that 62 percent of Internet users questioned make no distinction whatever between advertising and other information, and only 18 percent proved capable of telling which data were paid for by companies for their promotion and which were not. These numbers are impressive, especially in the light of others: 92 percent of users of search engines have full confidence in the results of their search, and 71 percent (users for less than five years) consider that information from this source is never biased in any way.

We should therefore keep our heads clear and not go into raptures over the abilities of capitalism, however energetic it may be, alone to create the best of all possible worlds. It may be suggested, in Google's defense, that the contracts it says it has signed with libraries that are collaborating with it are comparable to balanced contracts — "à l'européenne" — between two sectors, private and public, or at the very least between two disinterested (not-for-profit) parties. Although the relevant universities are largely free of state control, American taxpayers delegate to them, as it were, by means of fiscal incentives, responsibility for supporting a collective interest that partly escapes the influence of the market—and the same can be said of the very powerful cultural foundations on that side of the Atlantic.

Yes, but look at the inequality of the agreement. Libraries, in the name of their mission to disseminate a cultural heritage, generously provide the material to be digitized and the knowledge to be disseminated. Despite the false appearance of gratuitousness, the private sector reaps the profits by indirectly selling the use of these books through the advertising exposure that occurs with each hit, and also by global exposure. The company expects this increasingly lucrative business, thanks to Google Book Search, to have an impact on its entire commercial offering. Naturally, what remains of such profits, after distribution to shareholders, will further accentuate the imbalance in favor of the private sector and reduce the influence of those institutions serving the common interest.

Let me be very clear: I don't reject the cooperation of multiple agents, regardless of the sector they belong to. On the contrary, I call upon such cooperation wholeheartedly. But another balance must be established, one that will be ensured by the participation of a large number of financially disinterested agents. Governments should intervene, to the same extent as they do in Europe, to encourage the proliferation of potential creativity. Let them do so through regulations and by judiciously entering into the fray. Let them collect contributions from companies willing to contribute to the budget, not for immediate profit, but to serve this multipolarity of cultures whose economies, over the long term, will necessarily be enhanced.

Make no mistake: without such determination, not only will the common interest be threatened, but we will also see the global scales, in this realm as in others, tip toward the hyperpower of a dominant civilization.

3

HYPERPOWER

Let us fight the United States, less by denouncing their sins against the world than by striving to appropriate their virtues and abilities. :: MICHEL CHEVALIER, *Lettres sur l'Amérique du Nord*, II, 34 (1836) ::

"If the market ruled as master, it would be the Americans who ruled as masters over the market," added de Gaulle, following his comments to Alain Peyrefitte quoted in chapter 2. "They are multinationals that are no more multinational than NATO. It's just a camouflage of American hegemony. If we follow the market blindly, we will find ourselves colonized by the Americans. We Europeans will no longer exist."

The United States is a great country. Its affinities with our own history and culture are many, and we gladly acknowledge them. We share a legacy of battles fought together, a legacy embodied by Lafayette, Rochambeau, Franklin, Pershing and

Eisenhower—up to Kosovo and Afghanistan. We have never made war against each other.

And yet at each turning point in recent history, from the Monica affair, which absurdly weakened Bill Clinton in his international endeavors, to the reelection of George W. Bush, we have measured the profound differences in our collective sensibilities. To mention just a few random examples: the death penalty, the two million in American prisons, the relationship between religion and democracy, the role of money in American elections, the U.S. rejection of the Kyoto protocol on the emission of gases and the greenhouse effect, and rejection of the international criminal court to judge crimes against humanity. I may add, at the heart of the debate, Washington's recent refusal to sign the UNESCO motion on cultural diversity.

This of course concerns Europe's place in the world. But everyone else's, too. If we don't act, we can be sure that great powers influential over other regions of the planet won't hesitate to do so.

Most assuredly, our responsibility is that of Europe, the European Union calmly asserting its pride in being different and in bearing an alternate message to the rest of humanity. The EU knows, and France has no doubt of it, that the planet will be better off if we ensure an effective presence in behalf of Europe's own wisdom and of the civilization it embodies and promotes.

Nor is this all. Since it has fallen to us to advocate multilateralism, we must take into account similar aspirations from other regions of the world and make plans to cooperate with them. Otherwise, as during the invasion of Iraq, the dominant player in this respect (I'm speaking symbolically) won't be a body such as the United Nations or UNESCO; it will be the White House or the Pentagon, or at the very least the IMF or the World Bank, where American influence dominates.

I have observed that some people, such as Mitterrand's former adviser, Jacques Attali, deride this concern as "distressing provincialism" incapable of accepting "the formidable acceleration of globalization in progress" (*L'Express*, March 14 2005). This is a strange abdication, a strange ignorance of what the great movement in question calls for, provokes, and demands: the jealous preservation of differences so that the circulation of cultures and knowledge can remain fruitful.

India, China, the Arab World, Africa

We should fully expect that India and China, for their part, will soon react with an energy born of renewed ambitions. These two countries, in partnership with the Library of Alexandria and eight American universities, have established a digitization program for one million volumes (the Million Book Project). In both countries, ministries, research facilities, and universities are collaborating on the project. Twenty-two digitization centers focusing on works published in eleven of the eighteen official languages of India are already functioning in that country. In China, where eighteen digitization centers are operating, the government plays an even more important role, since it sees digitization as the means both to develop a cultural impetus and to reinforce its rigorous program of censorship. We know in passing that Google, following Yahoo, has agreed—to the indignation of many—to honor that censorship as the price of its extension into the Chinese market: this is how it "organizes the world's information."

It is important to note that these Asian programs have obtained solid financial backing from several American foundations, including Internet Archives and the Carnegie Mellon Libraries, which also provide technical advice. But this support comes precisely from organizations not seeking profit, quite unlike Google. (The Bibliothèque nationale is grateful to Mellon for a grant that enabled us to digitize the archives of Dunhuang, the town that was at the crossroads of the silk trade route and was explored by the great French Sinologist Paul Pelliot.) Is such assistance to the Indian and Chinese programs totally disinterested? We need to think about it. At least the choice of works to be digitized, pending further information, remains exclusively that of the countries concerned, and what is made available online will be free of any advertising support that would affect the hierarchy of what is offered.

There is nothing surprising in this activity by the two most populous nations in the world, in their wish not to see themselves lose their cultural heritage. Their growing mastery of new technologies and the low cost of labor in their countries are precious assets that will enable them to go forward in this adventure without qualms. They will soon, without any doubt, become the world's best digitizers. Indeed, they may already be so.

And so we should have no doubt that these two countries, with their many languages spoken by millions in remote areas, and their rich cultures teeming with oral and written tradition, will become our allies in this movement against a globalization that not only would prove unproductive but would encourage bleak standardization.

We should also mention the Arab world, so bruised in its collective pride. Upon arriving in Baghdad, the American troops chose to protect the Ministry of Oil rather than cultural establishments. The advance warnings of our American academic colleagues, knowledgeable specialists in these regions, went unheard. Hundreds of thousands of precious works of art and books were destroyed or looted. We must first hope, then expect, that the day will come when massive digitization, in a political climate that ensures those responsible full mastery over the selections and the way they are offered, will be organized to the benefit not only of the Arab world but of the Iranians and the Turks as well.

For the past three years I've been a member of the board of directors of the prestigious new Library of Alexandria, and I sa-

lute its director, Ismael Serageldin, for striving to make it the em-
bodiment, the focal point, of a liberal Islam compatible with the
spirit of the Enlightenment. For financial reasons he will not be
able to increase his holdings for some time. So he is wisely planning to investigate the prospects of the virtual. (As mentioned
in the Introduction, he had the first edition of this work translated into Arabic.) And we can well imagine that he will become
a leader in this field—on condition, of course, that he be guaranteed control over his domain; otherwise it might be difficult
for him to resist the obscurantist forces working against him.

In a broader perspective, we must also think of poor and un-
derdeveloped countries—notably in Africa. We are accountable
to them in this realm as in others. Yet no one should imagine an
absolute transparency creating perfect equality of opportunities
among individuals and peoples. That's for dreamers. For just
as there's a societal gap in France—narrowing it being more
difficult than naming it, of course—so too a digital gap could
develop around the planet. Worldwide, the gap will be geographical, to the detriment of southern countries; in Europe it
will be sociological, disadvantaging the poorest of our citizens.

The challenge, of course, is not simply the provision of
materials and the quality of connections; potential users need
to be trained so they can adapt, in terms of language as well
as computer jargon, to what they are offered. The ultimate
achievement would consist in providing all peoples, regardless of their wealth or poverty, the means to digitize their own
literary heritage, according to their own choices and their own
organization of the whole—and without pledging allegiance to
any particular digitization company.

Europe—the Courage to Be Different

I attended the speech Condoleezza Rice, the new American
secretary of state, gave in the large auditorium of the Institut

d'études politiques ("Sciences Po") in Paris on February 8,
2005. She arrived, smiling and determined, hoping to make us
forget the many harsh words she had spoken to us and to charm
France and Europe, which her government needed once again.
I thought those around me in the audience were too readily
succumbing to the relief of believing we were liked once again.
Beyond the pleasant feeling that George Bush and his entou-
rage, for the time being, wanted to tone down their "French
bashing" and their criticism of "old Europe," the basic feelings
and intentions of the speech were easily detected. Freedom was
brandished as the means to all happiness, the guarantee of all
equilibrium. On French soil, we have known the price of freedom for a long time. But its celebration by Rice turned it into
too great an abstraction, detached from economic interests,
social forces, and cultural factors unique to a nation.

And I thought of the word "liberal," which doesn't have the
same meaning in all languages. If it leads to the extreme Right
in Europe, the opposite of what it implies across the Atlantic,
it is because we know well that any freedom not channeled by
the law that moderates it can easily become corrupt; and also
because we know that other influences must come into play,
those of a legitimate government intervening as a regulator and
an agent, notably to serve cultural forces that couldn't prosper
without its support and guarantee.

We have not forgotten the absurd and revealing success in
the United States of Francis Fukuyama's words when immediately after the fall of the Berlin Wall he announced the "end of
history." A watered-down Hegelianism led him shamelessly to
proclaim that henceforth nothing would oppose the universal
triumph of the American model; it was boastful nonsense.

It was against this background that our questions were
spontaneously formulated when Google made its announcement to the world. To ask ourselves what that announcement
means to *us* is both justified and imperative, because it is rooted

in American capitalism as it functions today, and in American society as it has been conceived.

We love that great country for all the values it shares with us, and even for all the differences that stimulate our interest and our imagination. But for all that, we don't want it to assume for its own benefit, as a side effect of its dominance, unilateral control over the thinking of the world, even in the absence of any public outcry.

I know that Europeans often hear the reproof: "What? In every realm of culture, it was Europe that planted its seed in America, and America has managed to assimilate Europe's multiple abilities and sometimes its genius. America's triumph is fundamentally your own, so what are you complaining about? What are you worried about?" De Gaulle was fond of referring to America as "the daughter of Europe." No reasonable person can deny this. But nor can anyone deny that in the powerful melting pot into which those very contributions were poured, a different civilization was born. Not to mention the many other universal currents that converge upon the United States and eventually become powerful influences there.

During her visit to Sciences Po, Secretary of State Rice, anxious to win us over, cheerfully recalled her trip to Paris when she was traveling with the first President Bush, on July 14, 1989. Her speech included in passing an appropriate tribute to the similarities between our two great revolutions. And yet, while listening to her, I was reminded, unpleasantly, of a show Bob Hope had been recording for American TV on that same Bastille Day on the stage of the Théâtre des Champs-Elysées. It consisted of a series of sketches devoted to the Revolutionary period in France that we were then commemorating, sketches of stereotyped vulgarity stringing together the crudest clichés against the backdrop of the omnipresent guillotine. I also recalled that Simon Schama's book *Citizens*—which was a great success in the United States—so outrageously ratified the hostile, popularized ideology regarding the counterrevolutionaries, insensitive to the dazzling intuitions of the Convention, that no publisher in France would even consider a French translation.

I want our children, as they discover the French Revolution, at least to read Victor Hugo's *Quatre-vingt-treize*, or Jean Jaurès's *L'Histoire socialiste de la Révolution,* as well as Charles Dickens's very hostile *Tale of Two Cities*, or Baroness Orczy's *The Scarlet Pimpernel,* which I enjoyed as a child in the Nelson series (without harm, in my case, because I had antidotes): in the latter we saw ad nauseam those admirable British aristocrats tirelessly pulling their French peers from the bloody clutches of the Terrorists.

I'll be reminded that the Terror did exist. I don't want to hide that fact from anyone; I want merely to point out the complexity of its causes and the enlightening aspect of the Revolution until Thermidor, and, later, who it was that overthrew members of the Convention.

Again, I'll be told that Google won't be censoring the works of Victor Hugo or Jaurès, because they are among the titles in American libraries that will be digitized. True, but Google Book Search, according to a spontaneous (rather than malicious) process, is likely to list them far below many others..

Nor do I want the history of the Commune, of the separation of church and state, of a free France, or even of French colonization to be dealt with in such a fashion. And I'm pretty sure that every European country, including the former popular democracies that have joined us in the European Union, could offer similar examples. My readers in other countries may complete the list for what concerns them; it won't be difficult. To tell the truth, the same concern exists in the opposite direction, with respect to American history: the Cuban missile crisis or even September 11 should not be studied from American sources alone.

And naturally what is at stake also, and perhaps to an even greater extent, involves the rest of the world. If we in Europe remain somewhat protected by affinities in language, which will maintain European books on lists at a relatively high level, the same won't be true for countries beyond our two continents. Their works are bound to receive unbalanced treatment in favor of our own, and this will have an impact on future world history, which, in turn, will be profoundly influenced by our perception of it.

Look at an issue of great importance today. We know how Anglo-Saxon law competes with Latin law in international jurisdictions and in those of new nations. I don't want to see Anglo-Saxon law unduly favored by Google as a result of the hierarchy that will be spontaneously established on its lists. At the initiative of Jean-Noël Tronc, as chief of the bureau of Information Technologies under then prime minister Lionel Jospin, we were able to establish Légifrance, the largest free legal database in the world. What use will it be on an international scale if Google's search engine pushes its content way down the list?

In addition, we can't escape the domination of English here. It's one thing to accept that the simplified language that has emerged serves as a lingua franca, just as the watered-down Greek did in the Mediterranean basin during the Hellenistic period; it's quite another to praise its use unconditionally in the cultural and intellectual realms. Granted, many books written in other languages will be digitized, but according to the "gondola end" principle of selection, we will see a natural priority—probably in good faith and surely in good conscience—awarded to those written in English. We may note that currently Google is thinking about launching a system of automatic translation. It will be interesting to see how it works, and which language it turns to first.

Just for fun, we checked the Google.fr Web site's instructions, machine-translated from the English, for how to use Google Book Search. They were filled with gobbledygook, some of it hilarious. For example, in the phrase "a book whose content contains a match for your search terms," the English word "match" is rendered by *allumette*, the kind of match you strike.

What "Gondola End"?

The "gondola end" is the major risk we face. It involves the ranking—or hierarchy—of results in Google Book Search. It's the mode of selection that must be questioned, a selection based on the way the search engine functions.

Just as iron shavings are drawn to a magnet, a concentration of works is automatically accentuated in favor of the already known and established, through a natural cybernetics. Contrary to what is often believed, this doesn't occur because the number of hits constitutes a sort of permanent plebiscite, constantly challenging the hierarchy, such as *Fortune* magazine's list of the world's wealthiest people, which is always changing. The method is more complex and ingenious, though the results are similar.

The ranking is established by means of algorithmic calculation, a mathematical term defined as "a group of operational rules corresponding to a necessary sequence." In other words, in terms accessible to the common mortal, it's an automated process that yields a list of results. Upon what principle is it founded? Like the basic ingredient of Coca-Cola, it remains a well-guarded corporate secret. But we know that Google rankings are based principally (among other possible criteria) on the number of links each page has with others, the importance of each of these links being weighed by the number of links each has with still others—and there are billions. A supplementary parameter seems to consist of the number of times the searched-for term is found on a page.

An American academic friend of mine recently pointed out that if he wanted to find Colette's humorous nickname for Johann Sebastian Bach, all he had to do was type "Colette Bach" on Google and he would soon have his answer ("the divine sewing machine"). So the search engine functions as a handy encyclopedia. "But," he added, "if I search less specifically, looking for answers to a difficult question such as whether democratization favors equality or not, I'll have hundreds of thousands of pages to scan." This is where an understanding of the classification criteria becomes crucial. When Google classifies the results according to criteria of frequency and density of links, the pages most often recognized by the engine will in turn be more easily called up by other users clicking on links, and we can be sure (thanks to the principle of lending only to the rich) that the pages that are already overwhelmingly "selected" will continue to be so.

All of this virtual information is constantly being brewed in a global cauldron. The "Google Dance" (a nice term), which is reviewed at least once a month, demands an increasingly phenomenal power of calculation, entailing larger and larger investments. We are steeped in classic capitalist logic: you must spend money to make money.

Plainly, a system more refined than the mere counting of hits (which would obviously lend itself to cheating) is still a system in which success breeds success, at the expense of newcomers, minorities, marginals. It's a system that could seriously harm the balance and energy of world cultures unless other forces, eschewing market interests, intervene.

Let's not forget another significant effect: even assuming that no chronological criterion favoring the most recent information has been introduced into the algorithm (which isn't easy to determine, since the list we see to the left of the screen doesn't give the date of the proposed document), the latest facts will be favored because they call up the greatest number of links. Is updating of this kind productive? Sometimes, yes, but it also tends to make the field shallower, to discourage longevity, which is obviously harmful to any culture.

I don't deny that some European sites may take their place among the elite on a Web where content is searched, indexed, and ranked in this way. To take a notable example, when the Centre hospitalo-universitaire of Rouen pinpoints, catalogues, and classifies various health data in terms of their significance, pointing out other medical sites online and linking to them, it becomes a required destination, at least for Europe, and ensures itself a choice position on search engine lists, from which it is unlikely to be dislodged. Still, judging by what we know about search engines, such cases will no doubt remain rare.

As the software is publicly available, a European algorithm ought to be defined, so that it can be used knowledgeably, subjected to criticism, and eventually improved, by anyone who cares to. (We know that some Americans favor making algorithms patentable; the former French prime minister, Michel Rocard, along with other European parliamentarians in Brussels, rightly opposed that idea.) The development of an algorithm is not necessarily the prerogative of the public sector; private entrepreneurs (a notable precedent is the Linux operating system, the only real competitor of Microsoft's Windows) are already offering competing solutions. The state, however, should do the instigating. We must, in Europe and elsewhere, following a collective determination, exploit the diversity of individual initiatives in building a strategy to spread our shared knowledge.

THE DIFFICULTIES OF A
RESPONSE

The world is full of voices that have lost their face
And turn night and day looking for one.
:: JULES SUPERVIELLE, *Les Amis inconnus* ::

In order to respond peaceably to this enormous challenge, we
must return to the notion of freedom. But not just any freedom,
not the kind of freedom a fox enjoys in a chicken coop (the
image is a bit worn, but I can't think of any more appropriate
one), nor the kind Georges Clemenceau had in mind when at
the end of the nineteenth century, mocking the diehard liber-
als of his time, he conjured up the image of amputees racing
against thoroughbreds in the Grand Prix: "Good luck, and
may the best one win!"

I'm speaking of the freedom—which is by no means assured

merely by the dynamics of the market—of "small print-run" authors, of publishers with a small budget, and of cultures with small populations and a minority language. The freedom of all those who have contributed and will continue to contribute to the cultural wealth of Europe, yesterday, today, and tomorrow. I'm including the marginal sensibilities and minority cultures in the Anglo-American world as well.

There's also the issue of potential censorship, a major political concern for Europe. Earlier I spoke of Google's questionable compromise with Chinese leaders; yet Google reserves the right to ban a site anywhere if it finds that it has not respected a given condition for use—the site remains known to the company but can't be found by the search engine. It may not be too far-fetched to imagine that at a time of international confrontation we could be threatened, through misguided American patriotism, with a similar surveillance, exclusion, penalization of particular materials or of any book that might seem inappropriate to the American mainstream.

Already in 2002, Jonathan Zittrain and Benjamin Edelman of the Berkman Center for Internet and Society at Harvard Law School discovered that users of the German and French Google sites were being blocked, without any warning, from access to certain content. A company executive, Nate Tyler, then confirmed that several sites presented on Google.com were not available on Google.de or Google.fr: "To avoid legal liability," he explained, "we remove sites from Google.de search results pages that may conflict with German law. . . . As a matter of company policy we do not provide specific details about why or when we removed any one particular site from our index" (quoted by Declan McCullagh in "Google Excluding Controversial Sites, CNET News.com, October 23, 2002).

Cooperatives: Strengths and Limitations

How should we react? There can be no doubt: as we plan for future action, we must acknowledge the necessity for a powerful thrust toward digitization in Europe. It's a matter of culture—in other words, at this level, of politics. How can we get things moving? How can we accomplish the task?

In a world of almost infinite decentralized networks, we can dream of a concerted effort, supported by countless benevolent agents.

On February 17, 2005, I was explaining on a radio talk show on France Inter the ideas I'm defending here. A listener called in and suggested that it might be extremely useful to coordinate the efforts of a huge number of Internet users, and I later received several e-mail messages expressing the same thought. A network of cooperative activity, of a type that the Internet already promotes, might enable strong collective action in Europe and elsewhere, coordinated by a public authority. It might be possible, for example, to rally book lovers around a "Save a Book" campaign, each person contributing to safeguarding books in danger of demise as a result of the passing of time, the deterioration of the paper, or the wear of the binding. Volumes would be scanned by individuals for the benefit of all.

Don't laugh. The idea is already being carried out, thanks to lively minds, enormous energy, and generous sponsorship.

Project Gutenberg (www.gutenberg.org) stands out here as a prime example and deserves to be looked at more closely: first, because it originated in the United States and thus highlights the diversity of creative approaches inherent in American thinking; next, because it has survived so long, has seen excellent results, and has therefore gained the power to entice and instruct.

The project is headed by Michael Hart, whose messianic

yet pragmatic personality, tireless labor, and disinterestedness in the service of a pedagogic-moral vision of the world reminds us of Pierre Larousse in the nineteenth century when he established his admirable *Dictionnaire universel*. In July 1971, Hart launched a plan to disseminate, gratis, through electronic means, the greatest possible number of books in the public domain. Thus the first digital library was born. It really took off in the mid-1990s, when the Web began to be more widely used. It relies on the coordinated work of hundreds of volunteers worldwide, who scan books one by one and then control the results by correcting the text on the screen; a different person double-checks to ensure accuracy. Very old books that are difficult to scan can be keyed into a computer by hand. Today, no fewer than fifteen thousand books (two hundred of which are in French) can be downloaded for free in one's home.

Project Gutenberg has inspired emulators. In France, for example, we have the Association des Bibliophiles universels, housed, among other places, at the Conservatoire national des Arts et Métiers; the Ménestrel project, with a Web site dating back to 1998, which offers texts from the Middle Ages; and the Bibliothèque électronique in Lisieux, which already offers a considerable collection.

In the so-called exact sciences, using the work of multiple collaborators appears to be especially productive. A correspondent from Quebec, reacting to my article in *Le Monde*, wrote to me about SETI (Search for Extraterrestrial Intelligence): "American scientists have a project to systematically study all the radio frequencies of a portion of the visible sky, looking for potential extraterrestrial signals. Faced with the enormous scale of the task and the impossibility of finding a sufficiently powerful machine to accomplish their goals, they have created a small software program which, installed on the computers of individuals around the world, enables each Internet user to participate, at the user's own rhythm and according to his or her abilities, in the immense mass of calculations. According to the authors, this process is functioning very well and has even been extended to other fields of research." That's quite true: the same technique was used by the Généthon laboratory at the beginning of 2002 to compare all known proteins in the fight against genetic illnesses, thanks to the participation of seventy-five thousand Internet users who volunteered to put the unused power of their PCs "at the disposal" of the project via the Web.

For a European response to Google's challenge, might we put our trust in a cooperative principle of this kind? The strategy encounters two serious problems: first, exerting control over quality and accuracy and ensuring that the many diverse individuals involved in the project respect the standards and norms essential to maintaining consistency; second, and perhaps more important, scholarly harmonization of the contents and rigorous control over the data integrated into the project. There's a risk of uneven quality in the data submitted, and the weaknesses of a few contributions would be enough to undermine the whole.

Under these conditions, an undertaking of this kind, attractive as it appears, can hardly be pursued effectively other than within a restricted community capable of ensuring quality under cooperative control.

However much we like the idea of Wikipedia, the free, multilingual online encyclopedia founded in 2001, which already includes more than a million articles (a hundred thousand of which are in French) contributed cooperatively by Internet users themselves, it suffers from errors and simplistic entries because it lacks an established authority for validation: it's all the administrators can do to weed out certain submissions.

In December 2005, an article in *Nature* determined that Wikipedia was almost as reliable a source of information as *Encyclopedia Britannica*. Based on an evaluation of a sample of entries from each source, the *Nature* article revealed an average number of 3.86 errors per entry for Wikipedia, as opposed to 2.92 for *Britannica*. The president of *Britannica*, Jorge Cauz, noted that these numbers nonetheless represented a difference of 33 percent.

The *Nature* article was published at about the time we learned that John Seigenthaler, who once worked with Bobby Kennedy, was seeking damages for a scandalous biographical entry posted for several months on Wikipedia. According to the text, suspicions were raised about him concerning his possible role in the assassination of the two Kennedy brothers. The author of this very harmful lie (his name was Brian Chase, an employee in a small company in Nashville) turned himself in in a letter of apology, explaining it as a "bad joke." The episode highlighted the dangers of the Wikipedia model, and its founder, Jimmy Wales, set out immediately to improve the procedures of control and validation.

Public Money

With all this in mind, we don't see how we can proceed without the powerful assistance of public funding.

Let me be clear: a strictly budgetary vision of the situation would lead to nothing but inaction. It must be emphasized, however, that the economic prosperity of the whole of Europe, and the influence of its culture, will benefit from its role in this domain. When I was in charge of foreign trade in Edith Cresson's government in 1991–92, I quickly learned that the maxim "Interests will always compromise, but passions, never" was entirely false, because interests and passions were so intimately blended that you really couldn't distinguish their respective influences on our success in foreign markets. The cultural influence of France, like that of Europe in general, is not an end in itself; it also largely, if indirectly, affects our export capabilities. The causality may be indirect, but it's beyond doubt. Our leaders in Paris, Berlin, Rome, Madrid, and elsewhere, especially the EU authorities in Brussels, would do well to keep this in mind.

This same conviction should undergird a TV network outside of France, broadcasting French news internationally to the east, south and west, not only in French but also in Spanish, Arabic, and English—a project now launched under the name of Chaîne d'Information Internationale (CII). The same conviction, perhaps with necessary public financing, should have protected our prestigious photo agencies (Gamma, Sipa, etc.) from having their archives bought out by Corbis, a subsidiary of Microsoft, or by Getty—two organizations with powerful appetites. By virtue of that same conviction, Agence France Presse should have contracted years ago with other European national agencies to cover the costs of a bank of images for use in television, so that everything that concerns the rest of the world doesn't come exclusively from American sources—a dependence on another perspective, certainly honorable, but one that we shouldn't depend on exclusively and that would be enriched, furthermore, by competition with our own. The same conviction, finally, should have discouraged French television from reducing, as it did, the number of its correspondents abroad.

Obviously, such initiatives cost a lot of money. But there is no free lunch; citizens, and this is worth repeating, are always the ones who pay—if not as taxpayers, then as consumers. It's the channel selected that influences choice, either deliberately, or by the conscious or unconscious effect of the cultural climate. This is why we've waged a battle in France against corporate demagogues to defend the principle of paying a tax to watch TV—an amount comparable to what viewers in neighboring countries pay—which limits both the need for advertising income and its impact.

Image Mode, Text Mode, Metadata

This doesn't mean, of course, that we shouldn't make precise calculations. The alternative between image mode and text mode in digitization must be considered carefully. Image mode is an identical reproduction; text mode implies either rekeyboarding (typing) or scanning, operations that require rigorous quality control. Only text mode allows for appropriate indexing and improvement of the work.

Granted, it's primarily a question of money, since text mode, we are told, given current technology (which, however, is evolving rapidly) costs eight to ten times more than image mode. But should that intimidate us?

The choice of process should be adapted to the nature of the document. In the case of newspapers, for example, the advantage of reproducing the layout of the pages in image mode is immediately apparent, since the location of an article, its headline, and its dimensions are as important as its content and help us determine the significance of that content.

Gallica, developed relatively early and hence a pioneer in the field, has become difficult to navigate for current users. So we've decided that most of Gallica's contents currently only in image mode will be converted to text mode within the next few months, with the exception of early manuscripts or books that don't lend themselves to this change.

I should add that for the time being, as on other points, we don't really know Google's intentions in this regard. *Le Monde,* on March 5, 2005, ran an article by a reporter who had been dispatched to Google's headquarters in California. Not much was clarified. Having interviewed a company spokesperson, the reporter wrote that the company would of course adopt text mode, but in a weakened form that would not allow texts to be either downloaded or annotated. According to the article, Google hadn't ruled out mixing text mode and image mode.

This blending of the two systems, which seemed like a good idea, has been illustrated with the launching of Google Book Search in its "beta" version. Pages are presented with the searched-for terms highlighted on a facsimile of the original. Although the search, whether relevant or not for the user, benefits from the speed of Google's basic engine, the uneven and often disappointing quality of the digitization is striking and has disappointed those who have attempted to use this new service. Not only is it very difficult to read what appears on the screen—and the quality of the processes used for lasting digital conservation of works is also in question—but the underlying text mode is inadequate to enable proper indexing of the corpus. Here, as elsewhere, haste does a disservice to the initiative.

All of this must be studied in more depth. Much research is being done in France and elsewhere in Europe both on digitization and more specifically on metadata. This specialized term refers to everything that does not belong to the document itself as it is consulted in its original form but that is added to the document when it is put online.

Of prime importance is facility in locating a document on the Web and the ability to make the best use of it by means of the Internet. Gallica is planning to make further progress in this area so that those who are not yet aware of the extent of its offerings will be directed toward them by search engines. Everyone knows that if a book is misplaced on a library shelf, it might as well never have existed (our readers dread those "book missing" notices); we can't count on luck to restore it to a potential user.

Next, we must develop internal capabilities to locate content by enhancing the internal structure of documents with every possible point of reference so as to allow the maximum number of various uses: annotations specific to the user, glosses of every type, quotations, cross-references, and so on.

Without venturing too far into the technology, let's take a closer look at what's involved. The metadata must provide a range of information complementary to the document itself at the moment when it is reproduced digitally. Some such data are descriptive, the equivalent of bibliographic notices that one finds in classic card catalogs—title, name of the author(s), various references based on the classification developed manually by librarians (Dewey is the best known) or on keywords; other metadata pertains to the management of documents, recalling their legal status so as to protect the rights of authors, translators, and publishers; others describe the internal structure of a given document; still others describe the technical characteristics of the digitized data.

We may well expect that the differences between image and text modes will gradually diminish, because the former, much less expensive, will soon benefit from technological progress. The process known as OCR used in scanning should enable automatic analyses for indexing and searching by allowing the location of terms in their environment.

This reminds me of the distinction that was scrupulously made in the early 1990s, with respect to television, between direct and indirect satellite broadcasting. That distinction soon disappeared, so that the TDF1 and TDF2 satellites, which belonged to the first category, have wound up as rusted machines spinning around uselessly in space.

We should always maintain a balance between simplicity and complexity, as both tend to increase.

Everyone knows how simplicity relates to the success of personal computers in the past ten or fifteen years. And I have no desire, on a daily basis, to understand how mine works, anymore than I want to look under the hood of my car when it's running well.

But the greater the outward simplicity, the greater the inner complexity, dual characteristics of an instrument that should

henceforth be forged by computer specialists and librarians together—a tool that enables me, the user, though I've no understanding of its mechanism, to comfortably access documents,
today and in the future.

5

ONE EUROPEAN SEARCH ENGINE — OR SEVERAL?

The goals of the advertising business model do not always correspond to providing quality search to users. . . . For this reason and historical experience with other media, we expect that advertising funded search engines will be inherently biased towards the advertisers and away from the needs of the consumers. . . . But we believe the issue of advertising causes enough mixed incentives that it is crucial to have a competitive search engine that is transparent and in the academic realm.

:: SERGEY BRIN AND LARRY PAGE, "The Anatomy of a Large-Scale Hypertextual Web Search Engine" (1998) :: :

The Loftiest Aspiration

We now have to face a crucial decision that has gradually come into focus since the reality of Google Book Search was thrown into the public arena. In creating a European digital library, should Europe develop its own search engine—or more than one—that would enable it to remain globally competitive in this essential realm? Or should we focus our efforts on digitization alone, which would allow us to contract with preexisting engines, setting our own conditions? I opt for the first alternative—and we can already outline the thinking that should enable us to go in that direction. It would be intriguing to present the two founders of Google with this choice in the light of their comments eight years ago, quoted above. (That article has often been cited recently, and not without malice.)

The importance of the first alternative is underscored by France Inter's old slogan "Hear my difference." The major objection is its cost. Given the size of the investments already made by the big players, themselves supported by Wall Street, will Europeans be able to support projects and the endeavors that already exist in this realm under various names? Will we be able to develop others? Will we be able to meet the challenge in financial terms? The response must be positive if we truly value the cultural wealth of our continent. And there are several reasons to explore this possibility.

First, it is obvious—and the past year provides confirmation—that Europe possesses intellectual, scientific, and industrial capabilities that ask only for the opportunity to develop their potential in this field. A sure sign of this? The EU is never so firmly reinforced as when Berlin and Paris join together in the development of a new project. This is true of the Quaero program recently launched by the two governments, which I mentioned in the Introduction. Its goal is to develop a refined and specialized search engine. Thomson, France Télécom, and Bertelsmann would be the primary contractors. Some are already calling it the "Airbus of the Internet." Though geared primarily toward multimedia and moving images, it will necessarily overlap with Gallica's focus, and we will work very closely with its developers.

For the time being, Google, which according to various assessments is currently handling 75 percent of online requests in many countries, might believe that thanks to its ingenious technology, it's about to win out over its rivals, including Yahoo, Microsoft's MSN, and the engine launched in October 2003 by the online bookstore Amazon (www.A9.com). Google was introduced onto the stock market in August 2004, the value of the stock set at $85; it then made a stunning climb, reaching $450 a share, before declining sharply to less than $350 by mid-February 2006. But beyond the vagaries of the stock market, which may dampen unanimous praise of this new NASDAQ champion, its war chest remains considerable and, according to financial analysts, reached around $1.7 billion by the beginning of 2006.

There's no guarantee that the Google search engine, expanded well beyond its initial function and now a favored provider of a variety of services, with Google Book Search in the forefront, won't soon increase its costs. If so, Europeans will suffer, and those who, thanks to globalization, have taken the lead and already dominate the market will be the beneficiaries.

Google Is Not Immortal

So we have a choice. If Google reaches its goals at the expense of its current competition, it would be very good for Europe to re-create competition in a field in which technology and content, as they've done throughout history, so closely influence each other. In this way, both cultural freedom and the dynamic impulse of research would be maintained. But things may turn out differently. Neither Microsoft nor IBM, which are currently investing considerable sums in this sector ($150 million each), nor Yahoo, which is also making great efforts, nor even Amazon (which with the launching of its Search Inside the Book offers 33 million pages from 120,000 books), is ready to let go. We could also point to Ask Jeeves (now known as ASK.com), the young competitor that the billionaire Barry Diller bought in 2005, which is proving profitable and is already competing energetically with the big players. But we shouldn't forget what happened to Netscape (the Web browser), which everyone predicted would triumph but was ruined after Microsoft concentrated its efforts on Explorer. Still, in the event that Google were to fail (sudden, dramatic turnarounds are not unknown in capitalism), and the Europeans marched on, boldly and optimistically, their decision to set out on this course would be ratified, if only retrospectively.

In 2006 we can't help but be struck by the number of projects Google is showcasing, and this gigantic appetite will only be satisfied if its exceptional profitability continues to satisfy Wall Street. But there's no certainty whatever that it will continue, and the fluctuation that the company's stock has undergone should serve as a warning.

Behind its majesty, Google is hiding frailties, like any company founded on a (currently, at least) single, albeit profuse, activity, without any parent corporation or other major body to lean on. "If Google ever declared bankruptcy," mused Lise Bissonnette (president of Quebec's new Grande Bibliothèque) recently, "to whom would the new digitized legacy belong?" That's a good question: even if the digitized files were given to the libraries involved, those libraries would not necessarily have the right to put them back on the Web through a conduit other than Google; the opposite is just as likely. Such is the risk of conferring a public property to a private organization.

To this economic and industrial uncertainty can be added another—a legal uncertainty. If Google managed to crush its competitors, no one can be sure that its resulting status, however beneficial it might appear for the United States, wouldn't come under the scrutiny of antitrust law, the protection of competition being deeply rooted in American attitudes. High school students in France learn how the Sherman Act of 1890 and, even more, the Clayton Act of 1914 shielded the market against the effect of monopolies. That's why John Rockefeller had to dismantle his oil empire. More recently, Bill Gates had to bend to the same rule, at least for a small part of his activities. According to some, Google's situation is different, since the service it offers is touted as being free. A false gratuitousness, of course, as I've already pointed out, since we pay as consumers.

Let's imagine that in the meantime the growing powers of Asia—China and Japan—spurred by their linguistic specificity, were to develop their own search engine. Having missed its opportunity, Europe would have to swallow a bitter pill.

We must not allow ourselves an inferiority complex. A brilliant precedent should encourage us: Who would have thought, when the pan-European project leading to Airbus was launched in 1969, that it would achieve such success and that Boeing, attacked head-on, would have to resign itself to being beaten? Who would have predicted, when the European space launcher Ariane was announced by European Community ministers in 1973, that this ambitious project would flourish? Who would have foreseen that Galileo, the European system of radio-navigation and observation of the planet by satellites, would soon compete with the American GPS network?

To invalidate the comparison, some people argue that these are long-term projects, and that their stories are irrelevant to the world of the Internet. Even so, let's not be moths, mesmerized by a bright light. In this virtual world, too, we need the kind of long-term plans and broad thinking that can only be ensured when a nation instills the virtues of the long term into the superficial emotions of the here and now.

Longevity as an Obsession

We must consider the life of digital archives and their place in the technology, for although completely modern, they are as fragile as ancient books. All research must anticipate future evolutions, so as to ensure that the digitized texts or images can be reformatted without the original texts having to be re-input, thereby risking further deterioration. Digitization in itself offers no guarantee of longevity; it must constantly adapt to the pitiless changes of ongoing technology. And this fact must be an obsession for those in charge.

One of the weaknesses of Google's project is its apparent indifference to the question of long-term preservation and conservation. This, too, is an effect of the speed implicit in the project's commercial nature. The return on investment must be fast at all costs (and getting a seat on the Big Board won't encourage Google to concentrate on long-term archiving).

The instinct to preserve a cultural heritage, by contrast, is intrinsic to public institutions with a lofty mission, for which government funding ensures steady budgets or even, in the best of cases, periodic increases. I don't envy my colleague and friend Paul LeClerc, director of the New York Public Library, who is forced to spend most of his time soliciting donations. His job requires him to tread carefully, because his budget is subject to the goodwill of the library's wealthy benefactors.

Indeed, more research is already flourishing in Europe than in the United States with respect to the longevity of the digital medium, which concerns, of course, not just books and images, but sound archives and moving images as well, from radio and TV, overseen in France by the Institut national de l'audiovisuel.

Progress is already being seen thanks to various contributions from research facilities, public organizations such as the Centre national d'études spatiales, and private institutions such as those in medical imagery.

For its part, the Bibliothèque nationale has perfected a program called SPAR (système de préservation et d'archivage) to conserve digitized data so that they can remain not only in good condition but always communicable. This is indeed an area that needs a major collective effort in Europe, with Europe's unique resources guaranteeing continued vigilance.

It should be clear now, I think, why providing ourselves with a European search engine is feasible and would prove useful. But if we fail to demand it, if we resign ourselves to seeing Google or Microsoft triumph over weak rivals, without being dismantled by American or international regulation, then it's all the more important for Europe to pool its energies and embark on a vast plan to digitize our writings, our images, and our sounds—a plan that's exclusively our own.

6

ORGANIZING KNOWLEDGE

For this discovery of yours will create forgetfulness in the learner's souls, because they will not use their memories; they will trust to the external written characters and not remember of themselves. . . . you give your disciples not truth, but only the semblance of truth; they will be hearers of many things and will have learned nothing; they will appear to be omniscient and will generally know nothing; they will be tiresome company, having the show of wisdom without the reality."
:: PLATO, *Phaedrus*, translated by Benjamin Jowett ::

In my view, we should be less interested in the utopian dream of exhaustiveness than in aspiring to the richest, the most intelligent, the best organized, the most accessible of all possible selections. This view differs from what Google is proposing but is faithful to Plato when he shows Socrates evoking that Egyptian king who feared the perverse effects of the invention of writing.

The Harvest and the Display

We have become better aware recently of the obvious contrast in Google's system between, on the one hand, its capacity to "harvest" a huge quantity of sites and locate isolated passages in them in response to user queries, and, on the other, the quite primitive, crude, almost antediluvian nature of the mechanism that displays the requested information.

Anyone sitting in front of a computer screen can experience this contrast. The practical value of Google (or of any other search engine constructed similarly) is hard to judge, since the service is accompanied by no precise information about the limits of the search or the representativeness of the corpus in which it is carried out.

Just three days after Google's stunning proclamation in December 2004, Michael Gorman, president of the powerful American Library Association, reacted with a judicious distinction between information and knowledge. "The books in great libraries are much more than the sum of their parts," he wrote (*Los Angeles Times*, December 17, 2004). In other words, discovering books only through pages that are separated from one another and located by a search engine, according to the unique criteria of a search for related hits, is not necessarily a good way—and certainly not the most beneficial way—to approach books or make use of them. Books are designed, said Gorman, "to be read sequentially and cumulatively." And Google won't respond to that need; it's concerned only with keywords and with individual pages, not with works considered as wholes.

To pull up a page is something entirely different from pulling up a complete work. To quote Gorman from the same article: "A good scholarly book on, say, prisons in 19th century France goes well beyond simply supplying facts. Just imagine that book digitized and available for Googling. Google isn't saying exactly how such a search would work, but if it's anything like the current system, you might enter, say, 'Nantes+Prisons' and get back hundreds of thousands of 'hits.' Somewhere in those hundreds of thousands would be a reference to a paragraph or more in our book. If you found it, what would you do with it? Supposing it says, 'there were few murderers in the prisons of Nantes in 1874,' and gives you the source of the paragraph. That is all but useless. Absent a lot more searching, you have no idea whether there are other references to the subject in the book, and the 'information' you have found is almost meaningless out of context."

Gorman's concern is fundamental for the future of culture and for its dissemination in the world, once the technological progress enabling us to grasp digitally a large part of humanity's legacy in its printed form has been firmly established. What is more, this gnawing issue goes beyond the subject of the present book. It's now relevant to everything that circulates on the Web and to all the material from which search engines derive their information.

Take the incredible profusion of images, for example. Things have come a very long way since the Byzantine Empire (during the sixth to the eighth centuries of our era) was torn apart, at the cost of thousands of lives, by the conflict between those who refused any representation of God, Christ, or the saints, and those who defended such images or even demanded them as essential elements of their faith and evangelization. At the time, the images at issue consisted of rare paintings and sculptures in places of worship, miniatures of manuscripts that seldom left the royal court, presbyteries, or monasteries. By looking back, for a moment, on that period in history, we can better appreciate the vast number of images, fixed or moving, that are currently produced every day around the world and the almost limitless reproduction of all works of art.

Also to be considered are countless public and private archives that have resisted the perils of decay or loss through the centuries and that increase enormously from year to year, whether in parchment, paper, or—today—electronic form.

A final major concern is the Web's memory, which national institutions, depending on their mission, will be ever more committed to perpetuating, and which is rapidly assuming phenomenal dimensions. The archiving and conservation of Web sites to satisfy the curiosity of generations to come is already preoccupying most countries that can afford to assume the cost. Almost a dozen national libraries (those of Australia, Canada, Denmark, the United States, Finland, France, Great Britain, Iceland, Italy, Norway and Sweden) have recently formed a consortium for the purpose of sharing such a project, combining their abilities and their experiences. They are working with Internet Archive, a company created by Brewster Kähle, who conceived the brilliant idea of gathering a large part of what has been published on the Web since 1996. So the race is on between the gigantic expansion that must be safeguarded and the advance of technology that will allow it. Even if we have to give up the dream of exhaustiveness (which copyright registration, for all its rigors, has never been able to ensure), we can reasonably assume, barring a universal catastrophe, that the gamble will pay off.

Disorganized Bulk—an Absolute Danger

The enemy is clear: massive amounts of disorganized information. The progress of civilization can be defined, among other things, as the reduction of the forces of chance in favor of thinking that is enriched by organized knowledge. True, we know the pleasures of an unexpected encounter in leafing through a book, of discovering a new TV program while channel surfing, and of finding what surfing the Web can unexpectedly offer. We can be enriched serendipitously. But these small pleasures are worthwhile only if they fall on the fertile ground of an organized mind, if they are examined closely by a mind formed by effective training. Otherwise, since we are powerless to accommodate every fact, there would be only anarchy of thought and impediments to action.

At the beginning of this book I spoke of the hope that the Web, on a global level, might reduce inequalities of knowledge. Disorganized information, however, if it dominates, will actually increase those inequalities. Like the language of Aesop, like all the media, the Internet is highly ambivalent, and notably in this respect.

A brief return to Gutenberg's invention is enlightening. The printing press has not only been a powerful disseminator of knowledge; it also gave rise to the table of contents and the index, major improvements on earlier books.

We must now confront a challenge of another dimension. At the heart of this crushing mass of data we must determine the loyalties, the claims, and the standards to be followed as we select; for we no longer want to leave selection to chance. Accessibility to everything without Ariadne's thread to guide our curiosity may cause us to lose our way. The fantasy of exhaustiveness dissipates in the need for choices. In the future, in the age of mass information, selection will be crucial to every dominant and productive culture.

Let's consider the way a reader might use a traditional library, in which he or she is at liberty to wander around. The library's organizing principle is seen in the way the books are arranged on the shelves, an arrangement that strongly influences what the reader might find. Imagination is not inhibited but stimulated. The project, the reader's questions and hypotheses, engage in a productive dialogue with books grouped earlier by others, following well thought-out and long-matured principles. These principles are, of course, always somewhat arbitrary; their development is necessarily outdated; their justification is temporary, in the endless flow of knowledge; but they result from an attentive thought process, and above all they are explicit and well grounded.

And this is exactly the sort of system that should be transposed onto a virtual library, whatever it might be. Hasty classification of a list, following obscure criteria of classification, must be replaced by a whole range of modes, classification modes for responses and presentation modes for results, to allow for many different uses.

Transparency, Flexibility, and Rigor

Also in the tradition of good librarianship is transparency in dealing with information providers. What constitutes one of the essential generosities of the Web, from its beginnings, is the transparency ensured notably by "free software" and "open sources," respect for which has almost become a religion for some.

A dialogue must be established with Internet users that will enable them to determine the importance of each response they receive and to submit what is offered to them to their own critical—and lucid—point of view. A process of "questions/responses," currently being developed in many libraries, could be developed for the Internet that not only would guide users' specific research on a given subject but, inversely, would help to improve the organizing principles of the corpuses or the paths that allow users to navigate them.

A system for organizing knowledge should never be immutable. In this regard we are breaking away from traditional libraries, which preserve works on paper. Those libraries necessarily arrange their holdings on shelves and rarely alter them, whereas the arrangement of digital stock can be lively and changing. It can also, using the metadata that accompany each document, benefit from innovating manners of presentation, in the form of virtual graphs or maps, for example.

There's nothing utopian here. Imagination and determination are needed. Some Web sites already offer examples, such as the French Kartoo.com, which provides "conceptual maps," helping the user to navigate: a click on a "concept" highlights it on the screen and organizes a series of linked sites around it. And there is the American Clusty.com, which posts a list of answers organized in files in an "order of relevance," which is also explained.

A final observation: maybe one of the reasons that the top managers of Google never seriously broach the question of how works to be digitized are chosen is that they maintain the conviction—or rather the illusion—that they can digitize all the books that have ever been printed since the time of Gutenberg. In this fantasy world, there would be no need to worry about selection, and the performance of the digital library would depend only on the quality of the search engine (or engines). But since this perspective is beyond what we can reasonably envision (Is this a bad thing?), we must find the means not only to furnish Internet users with organized knowledge but also to indicate its limitations. At the same time, we must signpost paths leading users to other resources, notably those of traditional libraries, thanks to helpful online catalogues that allow us to browse through them.

So we return to the conviction that runs through this book: the Internet, a new and prodigious vector of knowledge but by no means a substitute for others, must, to escape the arrogance of its youth, repeat the experiences of earlier media and enhance the value and benefit of its predecessors.

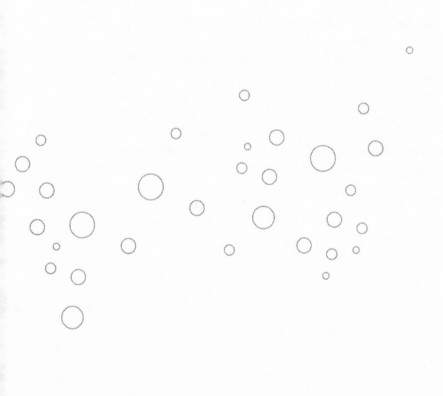

7

A CULTURAL PROJECT,
AN INDUSTRIAL PROJECT

To be fully enriched through reading, it is not enough to read; we must enter into the society of books, which then allow us to benefit from all their associations, introducing us to them, on and on, forever. :: JULIEN GRACQ, *Carnets du Grand Chemin* ::

In finishing, we should look at the broad outlines of the cultural, intellectual, and hence political project that should emerge from the thoughts that have just been presented. The project concerns Europe, of course, but I must assert once again that it will be at the service of the entire planet.

After an energetic start in 2006, some hundreds of thousands of books, not counting the newspapers that people in some countries would like to see digitized, are likely to be put online throughout Europe as early as 2007. After that, a yearly addition of five hundred thousand to a million works for the whole continent appears quite reasonable.

It's true that this estimate is below the gargantuan figures proudly announced by Google in December 2004. But since Google can't yet guarantee the achievement of its own lofty goals, I think I've shown that an obsession with numbers should give way to preoccupations with quality.

The plan will have to be carried out at a pace quite different from what we have seen so far, however meritorious our recent experiences may be. A strict timetable will be imposed, which all participants must follow, in conformity with a program to be defined by common agreement among as many EU member nations as possible, specifying priorities and the order in which tasks are to be accomplished.

Those who are concerned about an excessive governmental role, who fear that politics may corrupt certain choices that are made, must have their minds put at rest. Their concern seems groundless, especially if the effort is concentrated around cultural life understood in the broadest sense (never forgetting the political consequences and the indirect economic benefits that may result). It's a question of organization and making a clear distinction between two objectives.

Two Facets of the Same Aspiration

In the first place, the project will be an industrial one. Every stage of the project (as in the development of search engines) calls upon state-of-the-art technological progress: the logistics of handling books, digitization systems, procedures for classifying documents, and so on. The impetus of European political authorities will be needed, with the private sector having free access to the initiative and contributing its creativity. As in all scientific research, it would be extremely difficult as well as dangerous to lay out precise paths and set strict priorities in advance.

During a vigorous research and development stage, participants will be encouraged to organize or coordinate research into all the relevant evolving technology. There's plenty of evidence that our European teams are highly talented. One incentive to stay the course is that the technological advances required by the project will also serve economic and strategic goals.

Since the present book first appeared in France, we at the Bibliothèque nationale have been impressed by the number of institutions, large and small, that have indicated to us their ability and eagerness, their conviction, that they could devise and promote innovative technology to further this great undertaking. How can we doubt that once the sifting is done, these efforts will be beneficial to the economy at large, in Europe and elsewhere?

The other facet is a cultural one, responding to the essential question of how we can make our cultural wealth available, have it intelligently selected and usefully organized into a corpus. Here again, the government, taking care not to stifle imagination or inhibit civic efforts, must be the driving force. Of course, we can't allow politicians to involve themselves directly with content; nor do I think they would want to. But it will be their job to define a regulatory organization, to channel the creativity of the system while protecting it against corruption.

The task is dual. We must first establish, publish, and develop the list of what is to be digitized, determining the mode best adapted to the different types of documents and to the allocated resources.

We won't be starting from scratch. Film libraries, for example, are taking a system of this kind under increasingly serious consideration, as was shown by the European gatherings we organized at the beginning of 2005 at the Bibliothèque nationale, in cooperation with the Bibliothèque du film (BIFI).

I once presided, at the request of the president of the Institut national de l'audiovisuel, over a committee assigned to discuss the choices that should be made to best safeguard the unparalleled cultural wealth, including the archives of radio and television, granted by law to the Institut. We convened a similar committee at the Bibliothèque nationale to establish, under my initiative, an ad hoc documentary charter for Gallica. This is not a model, but it may serve as a source of inspiration.

What parameters of selection should be considered? The rarity of the document and its fragility, of course, but also its potential utility to researchers, its relevance in promoting the influence of Europe, and, above all, the place it occupies in a whole, in a "block of knowledge," the whole obviously being greater than the sum of its parts. That these concerns are sometimes contradictory makes it all the more interesting.

In practical terms, what criteria will govern the decision to digitize certain works? With respect to the vast legacy of works now in the public domain, that is, those published before 1923 in the United States (1930 in France), we at the Bibliothèque nationale think we should favor the great founding texts of our civilization, drawing from each of our countries: encyclopedias; journals of scholarly societies; major writings that have contributed to the rise of democracy, to human rights, and to the recent unification of the Continent; writings that have fostered the development of literary, scientific, legal, and economic knowledge, as well as artistic creation. We should add to these, as I've already suggested, works that have appeared in numerous translations, thus attesting to their influence. The same guidelines, probably with less rigid specifications, can be followed for the more recent period.

National libraries have a central responsibility here, of course, but they must also rely on the experience of others (we make sure of this in France), by way of their various associations, as well as on archives and all institutions involved in preserving our national cultural heritage.

Publishers Are Essential

Above all, beyond the responsibilities to be assumed by public authorities, we must involve the whole range of those who deal with books. I'm thinking of authors, booksellers—along with the unions or associations that represent these groups—and, above all, publishers.

Publishers are called upon to play an essential role in the policy at issue here. They are accountable for the huge volume of books under copyright, as well as scholarly editions of early books, whose critical apparatus is protected by copyright. No success in this field is imaginable without the agreement of publishers or, just as important, their ideas and professional competence. Google has been entirely too dismissive of their concerns and is paying dearly for it.

Of primary import are the protection of the material and the moral and intellectual rights of the author (the latter rights, insufficiently defended in America, are fundamental in Europe). Placing entire books online, even if encoded, is a dangerous game. Google had the gall to digitize books and disseminate them, merely telling publishers that they could ask (after the fact!) to have them removed.

As for excerpts, Google assured publishers that they would serve as teasers, or incentives, and that many readers, enticed by the excerpts, would hurry to buy the book in question. Faced with this situation, publishers as well as authors and booksellers should be the ones to judge whether this teaser effect is stronger than the opposite: a freely offered excerpt containing a lot of information discouraging someone from buying the book. Furthermore, copyright protection is easy to get around for any Internet user with some knowledge of pirating techniques. And legal experts generally agree that the act of making a copy, beyond the traditional right to quote a dozen lines or so without permission, itself constitutes infringement.

As elsewhere, the errors (I'm speaking euphemistically) committed by Google are instructive. Whatever it does, we should do the opposite.

For that part of the heritage of humanity still protected by copyright, we must put publishing at the heart of our planning and action. Along with publishers, we must devise several strategies: one for technical protection against pirating; one for the development of effective "micro-payment" techniques so that the costs of collection don't eat too much into the yield expected; one for permanence of digitization and metadata over the long term; and one for determining a balance—of which publishers are, after all, the only judges—between what they want to offer online and what they prefer to sell in a traditional form. Defending and promoting the traditional bookstore, with its essential cultural role, is an important element in that decision.

Discussions have already begun among those involved in France and elsewhere in Europe. We have noted with interest that a publishing union in Germany, the Börsenverein, has already sketched out an ambitious plan called Volltextsuche Online.

This is a good place to point out that as progress is made from one country to another, each must take the idiosyncrasies of the others into account—but with attentive cooperation.

What Structure? What Budget?

We may assume that in the EU countries that choose to come together in this adventure, scholarly councils will deal with the precise choice of works to be digitized, within a jointly defined framework.

These councils will focus primarily on their national legacy. Led by major intellectuals who have an international presence, all should be constituted in a similar manner. Along with librarians, the councils will include conservators, scholars from all fields, and eminent specialists in computer science; there must also be representatives from the many existing digitization initiatives.

The councils will be represented by delegates to a pan-European body. This body, which will probably be known as an agency or a common interest group—will be in intimate contact with the bureau of the Conference of European National Librarians. Overseeing the councils from Brussels, it will determine broad guidelines for a collective strategy to achieve coordination, encouraging decisions that preserve the record of exchanges between nations. It will no doubt be guided and inspired by the age of humanism and of the Enlightenment; this should protect it from any skepticism or discouragement.

It will be within this agency that the organization of knowledge into a corpus is debated, responding to the constant worry about disorganized information, the danger of dispersing knowledge into the void.

An important part of the agency's mission will be to connect and engage all existing resources—libraries, national archives, and universities, among others. For several years the Bibliothèque nationale, with its policy of "associated poles," has been experiencing and promoting the advantages of a dual conservation of cultural wealth, one digital, the other traditional—electronic as well as paper collections. This diversity, encouraged, coordinated, and standardized, will be both faithful to the specific genius of the Web and strengthened by a collective effort.

Will the money be there? In other essential sectors, the combined will of EU member nations has managed to mobilize the necessary funds. In financing its own plan, Google suggested a cost of $150 million to $200 million. Let's look at some comparable estimates: Brussels is going to allocate 190 million euros for the maintenance and development of naval construction in France and Spain, or 25 million euros annually for six years, and 20 million for two. The Média-plus program, for the period 2001–6, requires 600 million euros over five years to support film and TV. We might expect digitization projects to have been included among the plans and thematics revealed in the report "Pour une nouvelle politique industrielle," recently published in France by Jean-Louis Beffa; the report calls for "programs for innovation" that might require as much as 150 million euros in public financing over five years.

Besides money from taxes, we should consider turning to the private sector for funding—and not just to individual donors. The fact that the companies involved might expect some return, whether in terms of money or image, doesn't bother me, because the activity in question will be within a framework dominated by a "double sector," in which commercial corruption will be prevented by public authority. Incentives will have to be thought up, procedures invented; we've had plenty of success along these lines in other realms.

We will then have the power to be on equal terms with Google Book Search (and with other search engines that may appear, in the United States or elsewhere), and to negotiate, if necessary, our presence among them in a way that responds to criteria favorable to the influence of Europe, today and for the long term.

Whether or not we end up with a European search engine, all European countries should make a determined effort to develop strong networks, so that energies are coordinated and mutually reinforced. We need portals (some, as I've said, already function and are invaluable) that are constantly maintained and scrutinized, in which all the digitized documents made available through the initiatives of various public and private institutions are connected with each other, inventoried, validated, and classified. These documents will thus be broadly and easily accessible, and the rights of authors and translators fully protected. Then, coming together on a European level, these various portals may one day be regrouped into a single, powerful, and majestic instrument.

CONCLUSION:
A BROADER PERSPECTIVE

A revolution postponed for one day may never occur.
:: DENIS DIDEROT, *Entretiens*, Chapter 6 ::

While skimming some of what has been said on Web pages in reaction to my January 2005 article in *Le Monde,* "Quand Google défie l'Europe," I found a rather revealing exchange. It concerned the meaning of the word *défie.* Someone rightly pointed out that the English word "defy," with which American reporters immediately rendered *défie,* connotes a kind of violence or aggressiveness that isn't implied by the French word. The right word in English is "challenge," which has a different implication, more sporting, more positive, more rewarding for both sides.

This linguistic misunderstanding brought home to me the necessity—and difficulty—of protecting oneself against "false friends," in other words, of respecting each people and each civilization within the nuances of its own genius. It's to this end, to collective resistance against the perils of a forced homogenization of cultures, that I call upon Europe to contribute.

But as I read that exchange on my computer screen, I also saw it as an opportunity to emphasize the tone I believe should characterize the collective effort we are undertaking: calm but determined. It would be both excessive and counterproductive to talk of a crusade or a culture war. To accuse Google or its rivals of hypocrisy or corruption would be unjust. They are playing their game, and it's the game of the economic environment in which they are prospering, the technology they are developing, the country in which they are living. It is up to us to assert our difference and to follow our own path in our own way.

We Europeans are a republic. Only the foundation of popular involvement will ensure success. When a civilization believes in itself, it has a duty to invent the means to survive and to widen its circle of influence. It performs this duty better if it fully understands what is at stake. This certainly isn't the prerogative of researchers or intellectuals. All Europeans are concerned. I'm thinking especially of the two pillars of democracy so important to our nineteenth-century forebears—schools and the press.

Today, journalists in all the media are led to the Internet by the demands of their professions; the polymorphous documentation that is available to them there enhances their reporting. They are not just looking for specific data to ensure factual precision in their articles. They are seeking information to round out the news, to diversify points of view in space and time. They then disseminate what they find. So the classification, organization, and multilateralism of documents (books, images, sounds, and so forth) that are offered to them are bound, when journalists use them, to have a profound impact on the press's influence on society.

The Internet will also be increasingly present in schools, furnishing an abundance of texts and illustrations to be discovered either directly by the students or via their instructors. But Google Book Search, even though its leaders have not yet publicly defined the details of their practices, already appears to be a poor model for schools, since it seems to lack any kind of classification established according to reasoned principles. It is imperative to accomplish what education hasn't managed to do with television: students must be given the intellectual tools to master the medium of the Internet; they must be taught to learn and not just to ingest masses of disparate and unvalidated information. And we must help their teachers by protecting them from disorganized information.

As for adult citizens, society at large, they will find our digitized collections indispensable instruments for maintaining perspective in the face of the bombardment of new information, which they themselves must place in context, classify, and weigh. Unless a culture organizes that information, society is condemned to accept the mere dissemination of information, harmful to intellectual clarity and to a rich and harmonious public life.

I'm not one of those who castigate television for appealing to emotion rather than reason; it supplies a huge quantity of news and facts through its programming and its various channels. Our ancestors would have been delighted to have TV, despite what those who praise a past embellished by nostalgia and seen in sepia might think. Nevertheless, the very nature of the medium, with respect to the major popular channels, orients programming toward those seeking instant gratification, as defined by polls and ratings.

At the same time, in the margins of this dominant conformism, there's an urgent need to encourage the continuing vitality of those data and opinions which, despite a small initial audience, may prepare the movements and strategies of the future and alone can limit the hegemonic tendency of the great media and large print runs.

The Internet is a world of decentralized networks and we should take advantage of that. But those networks are formed according to guiding principles that governments must encourage, influence, and regulate. Flexibility, reactiveness, freedom of imagination and creation are indispensable, but so are validation and oversight for the collective interest. The libertarian spirit that appeared intrinsic to the Internet in the beginning seems to be stepping back in favor of a better balance.

Europe can be great only if it cares about less fortunate peoples and gets involved in helping them. European youth is well aware of this, instinctively as well as intellectually. The plan I call for in these pages, ambitious as it may be, must be placed at the center of a wider duty: that of reducing the growing gap between the privileged and the underprivileged, the users and the unconnected, the rich and the poor of the Web. It's not simply a matter of the "information society" and the imbalance in the production and dissemination of information, which rightly preoccupied us during the 1970s. We need to enable disadvantaged peoples to collectively appropriate their past.

History is always constructed by "temporal layering," to borrow a term from Jacques Le Goff, in other words, by the superimposed rhythms of events whose intertwining describes each historical conjuncture and helps to define the scope of action to be taken by leaders and citizens.

In the short term, with Europe at a gloomy conjuncture, treading water, plagued by doubt, and tempted to give up on the Union, an initiative such as I've been describing could galvanize the public and lead to shared pride.

In the middle term, as our continent confronts difficulties of expansion and seeks collective undertakings, the initiative could foster political cohesion and facilitate the integration of new members into the Union.

In the long term, our project should ensure a more harmonious balance, to the benefit of the entire planet. We are not striving merely for a better digital library. After the collapse of Marxism, we have learned that cultural forces sometimes weigh more heavily than material interests on the course of history. We must therefore expect new ways of thinking about national dignity and cross-cultural influences, representations, and stereotypes.

We are dealing, ultimately, with a universal challenge. May we have the courage to respond.

TRANSLATOR'S AFTERWORD

I am grateful to have had the opportunity to translate Jean-Noël Jeanneney's little book into English, to make it available to Google's home audience. The questions and issues Jeanneney raises are crucial not just to Europeans but to all of us on this increasingly shrinking globe. Google is a remarkably effective search engine—very few people would argue with that claim; as a translator I rely on it to find elusive references, and sometimes even to translate an obscure word. But should Google, as a commercial enterprise, be primarily responsible for archiving and making available collections from our libraries and publishing houses? Or should we, like Jeanneney, demand wider participation from the public and private sectors in the inevitable digitizing and electronic dissemination of books and journals? As in any rousing eighteenth-century pamphlet, the questions raised are stimulating and controversial, and the answers rarely obvious and never easy.

The Internet has made the world smaller than anyone could have ever thought possible. But do we want that world to be commercially driven, uniform, monolingual, two-dimensional? As we know, Jeanneney responds with a resounding no. It is now our turn to reflect and to respond.

As a final note, I wish to thank Dan Lowe for his gracious help with the more technical computer terminology found in the text, and Margaret Mahan for her expert—and often entertaining!—editing of my translation.

Teresa Lavender Fagan